THE GREATEST FIRST BASEMEN OF ALL TIME

THE GREATEST FIRST BASEMEN OF ALL TIME

DONALD HONIG

CROWN PUBLISHERS, INC.
NEW YORK

Published by Crown Publishers, Inc., 225 Park Avenue South, New York, New York 10003 and represented in Canada by the Canadian MANDA Group

CROWN is a trademark of Crown Publishers, Inc.

Manufactured in the United States of America

Library of Congress Cataloging-in-Publication Data

Honig, Donald.
The greatest first basemen of all time.

1. Baseball players—United States—Biography.
I. Title.
GV865.A1H617 1988 796.357'092'2 [B] 87-22208

ISBN 0-517-56842-X

Design: Robert Aulicino

10 9 8 7 6 5 4 3 2 1

First Edition

For My Daughter,
Catherine

By Donald Honig

NONFICTION

Baseball When the Grass Was Real
Baseball Between the Lines
The Man in the Dugout
The October Heroes
The Image of Their Greatness (with Lawrence Ritter)
The 100 Greatest Baseball Players of All Time (with Lawrence Ritter)
The Brooklyn Dodgers: An Illustrated Tribute
The New York Yankees: An Illustrated History
Baseball's 10 Greatest Teams
The Los Angeles Dodgers: The First Quarter Century
The National League: An Illustrated History
The American League: An Illustrated History
The Boston Red Sox: An Illustrated Tribute
Baseball America
The New York Mets: The First Quarter Century
The World Series: An Illustrated History
Baseball in the '50s
The All-Star Game: An Illustrated History
Mays, Mantle, Snider: A Celebration
Baseball's Greatest First Basemen

FICTION

Sidewalk Caesar
Walk Like a Man
The Americans
Divide the Night
No Song to Sing
Judgment Night
The Love Thief
The Severith Style
Illusions
I Should Have Sold Petunias
The Last Great Season
Marching Home

CONTENTS

ACKNOWLEDGMENTS

The author would like to express his appreciation to the following for advice and encouragement extended during the writing of this book: Michael P. Aronstein, Stanley Honig, David Markson, Lawrence Ritter, Thomas Brookman, Louis Kiefer, Douglas Mulcahy, and Jeffrey Neuman. Also, a particular expression of gratitude is due William Deane, senior research associate at the National Baseball Hall of Fame and Museum.

INTRODUCTION

First base is one of baseball's glamor positions, the place where many of the game's mightiest power hitters have played. It is also a frequently maligned position, considered comparatively easy to play, and sometimes it is: who among us couldn't take a throw from the pitcher or a soft toss from the second baseman to make a putout? It is the pasture to which aging hitters with reduced mobility are sent, under the reasoning that here they and their petrifying gloves will do the least harm. Some baseball men, however, question the wisdom of the tradeoff: Doing the least harm at a position that has the capacity for doing enormous good simply is not smart baseball.

But first base is also a position most underrated and unappreciated in the difficulties it presents and for the variety of skills required to play it effectively. According to some of its practitioners, it is the most difficult assignment on the field. They cite the many throws coming at them from different angles, high and low and sometimes skidding or bouncing in the dirt. Then they must field every conceivable kind of batted ball, from line drives to scorching grounders to bunts to pop flies fair and foul, and in pursuit of the latter they face the hazards of box-seat railings and dugout roofs. They are also crucially involved in cutoffs and relays and rundowns. They must move quickly and think quickly, having to make almost intuitive decisions on whether to throw back to first or to second

or to third on a bunt, depending on the situation and on the speed of the various base runners. They have to be able to execute the 3–6–3 double play as well as make the feed to a pitcher running to cover the bag.

This compilation of "baseball's greatest first basemen" is predicated on statistics, opinions, memories, and, unavoidably, a light serving of bias. The selections were made exclusively from those who played the substantial portion of their careers in the twentieth century; consequently, those left unconsidered include some of the great players of the nineteenth century, most notably, perhaps, Cap Anson, Jake Beckley, and Dan Brouthers.

Another category involves those players who split their careers between first base and other positions. Stan Musial and Ernie Banks, for instance, played large parts of their careers at first, but for the purposes of this book are considered to be men of their original designations— the outfield for Musial, shortstop for Banks—the positions they played during their top seasons.

While many of the selections are self-evident, any list begins inevitably to narrow and become more debatable. Given the scope of close to a full century's worth of major-league first basemen, certain omissions can be as arguable as some of the inclusions. At the end of the book, some of these omissions are discussed briefly.

THE GREATEST FIRST BASEMEN OF ALL TIME

Frank Chance, Yankee manager, in 1913.

FRANK CHANCE

Frank Chance was the anchorman on the most famous double-play combination in baseball history. "Tinker to Evers to Chance" may not have been the smoothest or most gifted of DP acts, but it remains the only one to have been successfully celebrated in rhyme and meter, courtesy of New York journalist Franklin P. Adams in 1910:

> These are the saddest of possible words—
>   "Tinker to Evers to Chance."
> Trio of Bear Cubs and fleeter than birds—
>   "Tinker to Evers to Chance."
> Thoughtlessly pricking our gonfalon bubble,
> Making a Giant hit into a double,
> Words that are weighty with nothing but trouble—
>   "Tinker to Evers to Chance."

Chance was born in Fresno, California, on September 9, 1877. Aspiring to a career in dentistry, the young man enrolled at Washington College in Irvington. To defray expenses, he began playing semipro ball in the area. The man who was to become one of baseball's most famous first basemen started as a catcher. Word of his abilities drifted back east to Chicago, and in 1898 Chance was invited by the Cubs to report to their spring-training camp in West Baden Springs, Indiana. Reversing the historic pattern, Chance headed east to seek fame and fortune, and he soon forgot about cavities and extractions.

Chance apparently did not possess the kind of talent that made his arrival in his first major-league spring camp a historic one. What did impress everyone, however, was his physique. He was a tautly muscled, 190-pound six-footer (a large man in those days, when the average man was several inches shorter) and was quickly nicknamed "Husk." There was something else about the young man that was quickly noted and mentally filed—a certain prepossessing quality that, along with his obvious physical strength, spared him from the usual torments endured by rookies in those years.

1

Joe Tinker.

Frank
Chance.

"Chance soon proved that he could throw, run, and hit," one observer wrote. "But he had the blamedest habit of getting hurt. When he was given the opportunity to work behind the bat, he stopped the pitched balls with the ends of his fingers, the foul tips with his knees, and the wild pitches with the top of his head." But the rugged youngster "could take the punishment and come back for more."

It should be noted that coming back for more took inordinate stamina and resolve for a catcher in those days, before the advent of masks and when chest protectors were primitive and only lightly protective. Baseball was a much tougher game then, with tolerance for pain placed at high premium, and for a rookie—they were not particularly welcome in those years of 17-man rosters—to so markedly impress the regulars with his grit was highly unusual.

Though Chance was far from adept behind the plate, the Cubs felt he was good enough to serve as a backup catcher, and they kept him (Chance never played in the minor leagues). From 1898 through 1902 he was a part-timer. In 1901 the Cubs

Frank Chance swinging in the Polo Grounds, circa 1908.

began breaking in a new young catcher, Johnny Kling, and Chance was feeling a growing dissatisfaction with what he felt was a career in stagnation.

Nevertheless, he had been hitting acceptably when he got into the lineup, logging averages in the .280s, and the Cubs decided they wanted his bat in the game on a regular basis.

In 1903 Chance was given the first-base job, a move he at first resisted to the extent that he threatened to quit and return to California and go into business. He had wanted an opportunity to win the first-string catching job, but Kling had quickly developed into one of the best

catchers in the league, and Chance, a pragmatic sort, realized he was not going to be able to move Johnny aside. So Frank Chance became a first baseman.

It was the same year that Johnny Evers took over as Chicago's regular second baseman, and with Joe Tinker already established at shortstop, one of baseball's most celebrated trios was now in place.

Playing full-time, Chance responded with a .327 batting average and tied as stolen-base leader (with Brooklyn's Jimmy Sheckard) with 67. The following year he batted .310 and swiped 42 bases.

In 1905, Cubs manager Frank Selee left the team in mid-season because of illness, and the club appointed their twenty-seven-year-old first baseman to replace him. First baseman–manager Chance finished the season with a .316 batting average and a team poised at the brink of greatness.

Buoyed by a pitching staff that included Mordecai (Three Finger) Brown, Jack Pfiester, Ed Reulbach, and Orval Overall, the Cubs went on to take pennants in 1906, 1907, 1908, and 1910; the '06 club set a still-standing major-league record by winning 116 games. Chance, managing his first full season that year, set a good example by batting .319 and leading the league with 57 stolen bases. It wasn't long before he became known, somewhat elegantly, as "the Peerless Leader."

Johnny Evers.

In an article published in 1909, Chicago Cubs president Charles W. Murphy offered the following thoughts about his manager:

> He is serious and inspires players to their best efforts at all times. . . . Chance asks his players to do nothing that he is not himself willing to do. . . . A bad play on the field is not allowed to be passed over lightly. Mr. Ball Player is told that such a mistake must not occur again. And he is told about it in such a way that he will not soon forget it, either. . . . For a man who has been as successful as he has, Chance is very modest. There is not a constant obtrusion of self-esteem about him, and he has always been able to get his hat on without the use of a shoehorn. He

Philadelphia Athletics catcher Ira Thomas and Yankee skipper Frank Chance shaking hands on opening day 1914 at the Polo Grounds, where the Yankees played their home games until 1923.

has the heart of a child and the courage of a lion.

Chance was big and strong, batting cleanup for his club; but since he played in the era of the dead ball there is no telling how powerful a hitter he might have been had he played in the days of the lively ball. Swinging for the fences was pointless back then, and few batters tried it. Consequently, Chance hit a total of 20 home runs in his career, with six in 1904 his high (nine was tops in the league that year).

Since Chance broke in as a catcher, we know he could throw; because he twice led the league in stolen bases and stole over 400 lifetime, we know he could run; his batting averages speak for themselves; and he was by all accounts a good fielder. But he did have one serious shortcoming on a ball field—a difficulty in getting out of the way of high inside pitches. As a result, he was badly beaned on several occasions, injuries that left him deaf in one ear and afflicted with severe headaches, and that, after 1908, caused him to miss more and more playing time. There was even some speculation that the beanings led to his early death in 1924, a few days after his forty-seventh birthday.

Time in its passage marks the pages of history in abstruse ways, and today Frank Chance is remembered more as a manager and as a name in a quaint old piece of doggerel than as a player, but he was easily the National League's top first baseman through the first decade of the century, a baseball player of outstanding talent.

It might be worth quoting from an article written by Johnny Evers soon after he had replaced Chance as Cubs manager in 1912 (bearing in mind that the men

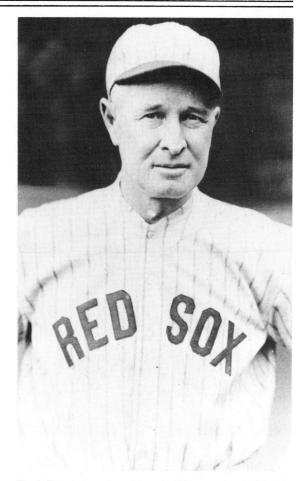

Red Sox manager Frank Chance in 1923.

were friends and that Johnny may have been feeling a bit self-conscious about getting the job). After praising Chance's leadership qualities, Johnny wrote:

> In the years when the Cubs machine was going at its best I do not think any player in the game with the exception of Ty Cobb did more really brilliant work for his club than Chance. He was a great batter, a great fielder, and a great base runner. He was brilliant in every department of the game, and in those years his all-around abilities were in my opinion matched by none.

Hal Chase in 1906.

HAL CHASE

One writer has called Hal Chase "the Benedict Arnold of baseball." In the context of American history, that's like being pressed by a branding iron; but if baseball, a history within a history, can have a deity (Babe Ruth), a Lincoln (Branch Rickey), a saint (Connie Mack), a crusader (Jackie Robinson), and various heroes noble and tragic, then it is entitled to at least one infamous archangel. Making it all the more poetic was the fact that Chase was, before the arrival of George Sisler, baseball's nonpareil first baseman; therefore, his descent from the sublime was considerable.

If Chase was a villain, then he was out of the classic mold. Contemporaries remembered him as charming, witty, well-spoken, and altogether an enjoyable companion—a man among men. Also a rogue among rogues: He was a gambler, a pool shark, a dead shot with a rifle, handy with his fists. Evidently, this rough customer, who had "red hair, sharp eyes, and a pugnacious jaw," did not arrive in the shadows via the high road.

On a ball field he was a dazzler, the slickest glove ever seen, touchstone for decades of first basemen to come, and, as long as there remained living witnesses, "the greatest fielder of them all." It was said that fans came to the Yankees' old Hilltop Park at Broadway and 165th Street just to watch Chase's wizardry around first base.

In a 1908 article, Chase was described as having "the easy disingenuous air of the man who is perfectly at peace with his surroundings and with life in general, the attitude of the happy-go-lucky individual who takes things as he finds them and can find gilded linings to every cloud." Chase was, said this writer, "the most famous player who ever graced the initial sack of any diamond, the one man in the game today a little better than any other who plays his position or who ever played it." Hal Chase was "the idol of Manhattan, the pride of a million small boys who gaze[d] in awe at his exploits."

Major-league baseball's most notorious character was born in Los Gatos, Califor-

7

A game in progress at Hilltop Park early in the century. The Yankees (in the field) are hosting the Chicago White Sox. Chase is playing first base. Note how far off the bag and close in he is.

nia, on February 13, 1883. He reached the big leagues via Los Angeles in the Pacific Coast League, landing with the Yankees (then known as the Highlanders) in 1905. The right-handed-hitting Chase (he threw with his left hand) batted .249 in his first season. Never a high-average hitter, he batted over .300 just five times in his 15-year career, which included a year and a half in the Federal League.

Chase rang up a .323 batting average in 1906, .315 in 1911, and .314 in his combined American League–Federal League year in 1914, led the National League in 1916 with a .339 mark while playing with Cincinnati, and hit .301 for a half year

with the Reds in 1918. He was probably a better hitter than his .291 lifetime average suggests, but we'll never know, because we'll never know when he was trying and when he wasn't.

But it wasn't Prince Hal's (that was the regal nickname his glove earned him) hitting that established his niche in baseball lore; it was rather his extraordinary fielding and his amoral behavior (he was described as having "a corkscrew brain").

The record books can tell us how hard and how often men who have passed from living memory hit the ball, but for knowledge of a player's agility and his skills with a glove we must rely on what amounts to folklore. Venerable witnesses who attended major-league baseball for 60 or 70 or 80 years have gone to their graves swearing that Hal Chase—the Prince Hal of their youth—was unmatched at first base. This assessment may be influenced by generational pride (each generation tends to hold that they alone have seen the "greatest,"), but the very fact of their stubborn judgment about Chase does tell us something.

Sportswriter Fred Lieb, who came to New York in 1911 and thereafter observed big-league baseball for nearly seven decades, wrote of Chase in his memoirs *Baseball As I Have Known It:*

> As a glove man (when the mood was on him), only Sisler and Terry have come close to him. His range was incredible because of his speed. No other first baseman played so far off the bag. As a man charging in on a bunt he was fantastic. I have seen him field bunts on the third-base side of an imaginary line between home plate and the pitching rubber, and make his left-handed whiplike throws to third, to second, or to first as the occasion required, all in one apparently seamless motion. He was speed and grace personified.

One writer remembered Chase making the following play: "The squeeze play was called for by the opposition, and Prince Hal scented the trick. He crept in while the pitcher was winding up. The base runner made a fast start, and the batter tapped the ball down the first-base line. Chase took it on one bound and dived through the air, touching the runner before he reached the plate."

Chase's ability at swooping in on bunts was of crucial importance in the dead-ball era, when the bunt was a frequently employed offensive weapon. Time and again, when one reads about Chase's unparalleled talents, their cutting edge is in nullifying bunts.

Another notable Chase quality was the amount of ground he covered, something he was able to achieve by playing farther off the bag than any other first baseman. His exceptional foot speed enabled him to get to the base in time to receive throws from his infielders and make the putout. Another aspect of the Chase performance had an element of the theatrical: He was noted for making easy plays look difficult and for snatching balls out of the air with one hand in an era of predominantly two-handed catches.

Chase's scintillating defensive skills were not confined solely to preventing the opposition from scoring; he was equally adept at deliberately misplaying balls, maneuvers he executed with such finesse that it was hard to tell whether he was trying or not.

They said he had "a corkscrew brain."

Chase with the Cincinnati Reds in 1916, the year he led the National League in batting.

"Eventually his reputation began to stink to high heaven," one old teammate recalled, "and that was the only way you could catch on to what he was doing. He was so damned smooth at everything that, if you didn't know what to look for, you wouldn't have known he was throwing games."

Fred Lieb gives one view of Chase earning a dishonest buck: "His neatest trick was to arrive at first base for a throw from another infielder just a split second too late." An infielder had to throw to the bag under the generally correct assumption that the first baseman would be there on time, particularly when the first baseman was Hal Chase. But if Chase had a

financial interest in the game's outcome, he could, by slowing his dash to the base by a split second, allow an accurately thrown ball to sail an inch or two out of reach. "He could do something like that," teammate Roger Peckinpaugh said years later with some bemusement, "and make it look so good, like he was trying his damnedest. Any way you look at him, he was the greatest—the greatest first baseman and the greatest scoundrel."

By 1913 Chase's defensive genius was legendary, even as his reputation became more malodorous. He was, next to Cobb, the league's biggest drawing card, a status that apparently gave him a certain immunity. In 1913 Frank Chance, now managing the Yankees, told several sportswriters (including Lieb) that Chase was throwing games. No newspaper would print the shocking accusation. According to Lieb, Chase was so highly prized a star that only the most concrete evidence would bring him down.

"Everybody knew it, everybody suspected it," Lieb said. "There were those who saw Chase associating with some of New York's most notorious gamblers, and it was common knowledge that he would bet against his own team. But he was just too popular a player for anyone to touch."

Those were the days before Judge Kenesaw Mountain Landis became baseball's almighty commissioner (it was, in fact, rogues like Chase that led to the hiring of Landis). Baseball was run by a three-man commission consisting of the league presidents and a club owner. Strict central authority was lacking. Chase was not the only player suspected of dumping games; he was, however, considered the most flagrant as well as the most dangerous, since he reportedly was not beyond asking a teammate to

With the Reds, at about the time he was making manager Christy Mathewson suspicious.

throw in with him and pick up a bit of extra money. Just how many players the insidious Chase may have contaminated is not known.

Frank Chance wanted no part of Prince Hal, and early in the 1913 season he saw to it that Chase was traded, to the White Sox. Supposedly, the White Sox were fully aware of Chase's antics but were willing to overlook them for the distinction of possessing him.

Well, they didn't possess him for very long. When a third major league, the Federal League, was formed in 1914 to compete with the existing majors, Chase, whose only loyalty seemed to be to his next whim, broke his contract and jumped to the new league, signing with the Buffalo club.

The Federal League turned out to be a momentary blip on the radar screen of sports history, fading away after two years. Its more talented players quickly found employment in the National and American leagues, with one notable exception. No one, it seemed, wanted Harold Harris Chase, just thirty-two years old and still considered unequaled around first base. No one in the American League, at any rate, where they'd had a bellyful of his shenanigans. In the National League, the Cincinnati Reds were naive or gullible enough to sign him; or maybe they were hoping to inspire redemption. Or maybe it was simply as Roger Peckinpaugh put it 60 years later, still unable to conceal his amused admiration for the old wizard: "Everybody knew he was a stinker. There was no way they couldn't have known by then. But I wasn't surprised when I heard that somebody still wanted him. That's how good he was. He was that damned good."

Cincinnati was rewarded with Chase's best season, in 1916. Hal won the National League batting title with a .339 average, leading a cynic to wonder if perhaps Chase was betting on his own team that year. Nevertheless, Chase's manager, none other than Christy Mathewson, citadel of all that was honorable and impeccable in baseball, doubted the fidelity of his enigmatic star. In fact, Christy had more than doubts; he told some members of the Cincinnati press and the National League's president John Heydler that Chase was throwing games.

The matter was about to boil over in 1918, but Mathewson joined the army that year and went to France. Heydler continued the investigation, but without Mathewson, who would have been quite a formidable witness, Prince Hal was able to slither off the hook. According to Lieb, Heydler said Chase was clearly guilty of betting against his own team, but, Lieb added, "I have no proof that will stand up in a court of law."

Chase was through in Cincinnati, but to the surprise and chagrin of many, who should offer him a contract for the 1919 season but New York Giants manager John McGraw. If there was a powder keg of baseball integrity, it was McGraw. John J. not only was aware of the Heydler investigation but also knew that the allegations against Chase had been brought by McGraw's closest friend in baseball, his one-time ace pitcher and

the man whom he regarded almost as a son, Christy Mathewson. Nevertheless, McGraw, like so many others, was beguiled by the silken talents of Hal Chase. And no doubt the fearsome, autocratic McGraw could not believe that Chase would dare commit any of his peccadillos under the keen and unforgiving eyes of John J. McGraw.

The Giants and Reds ran a close pennant race through the summer of 1919. By the middle of August, however, McGraw had seen enough. There had been some funny business in the infield, with the culprits third baseman Heinie Zimmerman and first baseman Hal Chase. "I heard about it a few years later, when I joined the team," third baseman Freddie Lindstrom said. "Nobody was too specific, and I didn't ask any questions. But I knew about Chase, and I didn't have to ask what was meant by 'funny business.' Apparently Hal Chase was absolutely incorrigible."

It was quietly announced that both Chase and Zimmerman had been suspended indefinitely. No charges were ever brought, and neither man ever challenged what amounted to a permanent expulsion from organized baseball.

At the age of thirty-six, Chase was through. His name surfaced again in 1920 during the investigation of the 1919 World Series scandal, when there were rumors that he had acted as a liaison between gamblers and some of the White Sox players who had thrown the Series to the Cincinnati Reds. Chase was never actually charged in the scandal, but there were plenty of knowing winks.

Prince Hal packed his gloves and spikes and drifted away, to the Southwest. There, getting games when he could, he appeared with semipro teams

Chase with the New York Giants in 1919, his final year in the big leagues.

in mining towns in Arizona and New Mexico, appearing, disappearing, reappearing, by all accounts his old congenial self but saying little, as befit a man with a past; we can assume that in the sullen, sun-baked towns of the old frontier he was asked few questions. In his forties he was still performing his dazzling pirouettes around first base, dancing across the hard and rocky diamonds and showing the locals the artistry that for years had drawn marveling fans to the big-league parks and created a legend that by then had become part of baseball folklore.

Apparently not the kind of man to spill any beans, Chase never publicly expressed any remorse over the shady byways he had pursued. Accordingly, he took it all to the grave with him, dying at the age of sixty-four, in Colusa, California, on May 18, 1947.

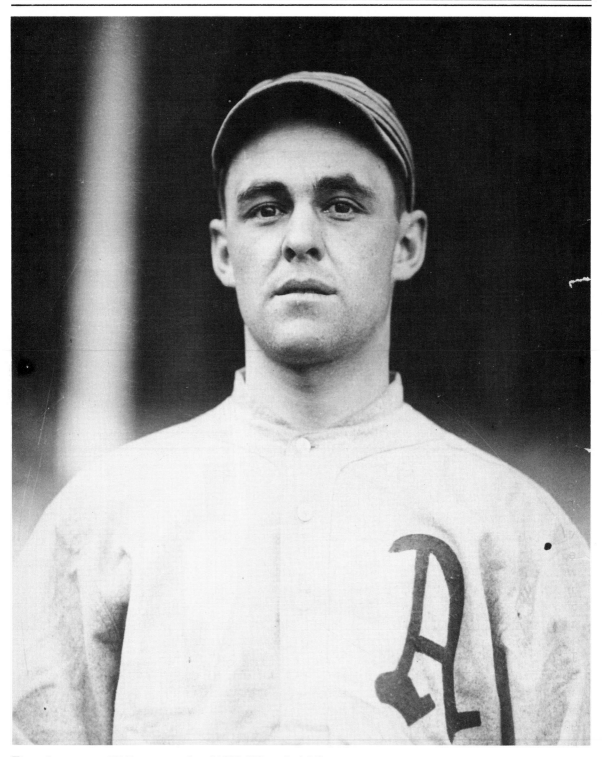

First baseman McInnis on the "$100,000 infield."

STUFFY McINNIS

Their nicknames were Stuffy, Cocky, Black Jack, and Home Run. Their last names were McInnis, Collins, Barry, and Baker, and they comprised either the most-famous or second-most-famous infield combination in baseball history, depending on how you feel about Tinker, Evers, and Chance, who had poetry going for them; but the other combination had money, or at least played under its banner, for they were known as "the $100,000 infield."

Now, that was a lot of money back then (we're talking about 1911, 1912, 1913), and it was not what they were being paid (no four infielders of that era made *that* much money), but owner Connie Mack had made the grand statement that he would not take $100,000 for them.

The first baseman on this munificently labeled infield was John Phalen McInnis, a native of Gloucester, Massachusetts, where he was born on September 19, 1890. Gloucester was then one of the great fishing ports in the United States. From its wharves sailing ships departed

to ply the waters of the Grand Banks and the Newfoundland Coast, returning with bounties of cod and hake and halibut. By 1913, however, the Massachusetts fishing port found itself being associated with Stuffy McInnis as much as with nets and trawl lines. That was the year that one writer declared McInnis "the greatest first baseman in the American League." The fact that Hal Chase, whom everyone pretty much agreed had set the standard around the bag, was still sparkingly active made the declaration a significant one.

The league's "greatest first baseman" entered pro ball with the Haverhill club of the New England League in 1908 as a second baseman, and major-league ball with the Philadelphia Athletics in 1909 as a shortstop.

Stuffy's rise to the big leagues was extraordinarily swift. He played just 51 games for Haverhill in 1908, batted .301, and was purchased by the Athletics. In 1909, Connie Mack took a liking to the eighteen-year-old youngster and kept

The eighteen-year-old rookie shortstop with the Philadelphia Athletics in 1909.

him with the A's. McInnis warmed the bench most of the season, getting into just a handful of games, all at shortstop, while Connie mulled over what to do with him. Frank Baker had third base nailed down, Jack Barry was a gifted young shortstop, and nobody was going to move Eddie Collins off second base.

Connie's first baseman was Harry Davis, a 15-year veteran nearing the end of the line; the skipper decided to make a first baseman of the gifted, versatile young McInnis.

By 1911 Stuffy was beginning to take over at first base, batting a solid .321 in his first full season, as the A's won the pennant. A year later he batted .327 (his all-time high), and then in 1913 continued to display the consistency that would mark his 19-year career, posting a .326 batting average as the A's took another pennant. In 1914 Stuffy helped the club to yet another flag with a .314 average.

McInnis, who was to become one of the finest fielding first basemen of his time, started slowly in this department, making bushels of errors during his first two seasons. By 1913, however, his .992 fielding average led American League first basemen and he was being compared to the incomparable Chase. "McInnis is not so flashy as Chase used to be," one contemporary journalist wrote, "but it is doubtful if he is not fully as effective. He certainly covers as much ground and fields with as much precision and ability as any other performer in the game."

In the current era of routinely made one-handed plays, it is interesting to quote another eyewitness to McInnis's style of play, which was considered radical back in those days of sunshine and $100,000 infields.

"Where the ordinary first baseman

reaches for the ball with both hands, McInnis uses but one. He can field as well with one hand as he can with both. He is one of the few players who are natural one-handed fielders."

In comparing the fielding styles of Chase and McInnis, another writer gave some insight into the executions of Prince Hal: "Where the average player fields with one hand, he is supposed to be making a grandstand play. Chase was very fond of these plays, plays which another

McInnis with the Red Sox in 1918.

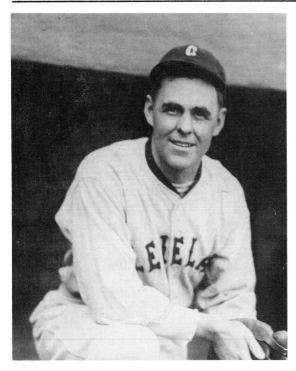

With Cleveland in 1922.

"All next season," Dykes said, "whenever I got down to first base and wanted to stir him up, I'd say, 'You know, Stuffy, that really wasn't an error. I was safe either way, whether you dropped it or not.' He'd press his lips together and make believe he wasn't listening. Finally one day, without looking at me, he said out of the corner of his mouth, 'Shut up, Dykes. You just shut up about it. If you mention that error one more time, so help me, Dykes, so help me . . .' "

McInnis was traded to Cleveland in 1923 and led the league in fielding again (it was the fifth time), committing just five errors this season, while batting .305, making it nine years out of the last 12 he had cleared the .300 mark (in two of his misses he was at .295 and .297).

first baseman would have made equally well, but Chase loved to do things in a way that made them appear difficult, to invest them with the charm of the flashy, the unusual. In McInnis' case there is nothing affected in his one-hand work."

After nine years with the Athletics, McInnis was traded to the Boston Red Sox in 1918, just in time to head into another World Series. He played with the Sox until 1921. In 1921 he put in a most spectacular year with the glove, making just one error in 152 games and ringing up a near-perfect .999 fielding percentage.

The single error came early in the season, at Fenway Park. With the Athletics' Jimmy Dykes leading off first, the Red Sox catcher fired down to pick him off. McInnis dropped the ball and was charged with an error. Dykes, a most mischievous character, remembered it well.

McInnis with the Pirates in 1925, the year he batted .368.

In 1923 he was waived to the Boston Braves and continued poking National League pitchers with his usual regularity, batting .315 and .291. In 1925 he was released and signed with the Pirates as a part-timer. In 59 games he batted a robust .368 and helped the team win the pennant, getting into his fifth and final World Series. He closed out his big-league career two years later as manager of the Philadelphia Phillies.

Never a power hitter—he had just 20 home runs in his career—McInnis was a nearly flawless contact hitter. In 1921 he struck out nine times in 584 at bats and a year later five times in 537 at bats. His lifetime batting average is .308. It was as a fielder, however, that McInnis made his mark. His .999 fielding average in 1921 remains the American League record for first basemen. From May 31, 1921, through June 2, 1922, in a total of 163 games, McInnis handled without error 1,700 consecutive chances, a major-league record.

Nearly two decades in the major leagues and hardly a story or anecdote left behind. Stuffy's passage across the diamonds and into the record books was one of quiet efficiency. We do know, however, that he was a gentleman, in a day and age when that was a distinction worth noting. In 1913 it was written of John Phalen McInnis: "Ballplayers as a class are careless in their speech. After all the years of regenerating influence the National Game is still a bit rough on the edges. The players who are gentlemanly at all times are in the great minority. . . . McInnis is one of this select few players who are a credit to their profession in every particular. Furthermore, he never uses tobacco or liquor in any form."

Manager of the Philadelphia Phillies in 1927.

George Sisler in the early 1920s.

GEORGE SISLER

Even by the elevated batting standards of the 1920s, what George Sisler did early in that hit-happy decade remains remarkable. Branch Rickey described the Sisler of 1920 as "the greatest ballplayer that ever lived." In a year of pure, shimmering magic the St. Louis Browns' twenty-seven-year-old first baseman batted .407 and rang up what has remained throughout the rest of the century the all-time record for hits in a single season, 257—86 of them for extra bases (49 doubles, 18 triples, 19 home runs)—while fielding brilliantly.

If the Sisler of 1920 was the greatest ballplayer that ever lived, then the Sisler of 1922 was also a highly noticeable performer. He collected 246 hits and batted .420, achieving the second-highest batting average in American League history (topped only by Nap Lajoie's .422 in 1903). That was also the year he hit in 41 consecutive games, breaking Ty Cobb's American League record by one. It was Sisler's record that Joe DiMaggio broke in 1941 on his way to his landmark 56-game hitting streak.

No city in major-league baseball ever saw such a tandem as St. Louis did in 1922—Sisler batting .420 for the Browns and Rogers Hornsby .401 for the Cardinals. Neither club won a pennant, though the Browns did come heartbreakingly close, losing out by a single game to Babe Ruth and the Yankees. This was as close as Sisler was to come to a World Series in his 15-year career, leaving him among those great players who never were with a pennant winner, a list that includes such luminaries as Harry Heilmann, Ted Lyons, Luke Appling, Ernie Banks, Ralph Kiner, and others.

Sisler was a ballplayer of glittering brilliance, offensively and defensively (he also led the league in stolen bases four times). He was, in fact, generally acclaimed the greatest of all first basemen until nudged aside by the power hitting of Lou Gehrig.

Like Gehrig, Sisler was a reserved, unassuming man, playing day in and day out with barely a rustle of temperament. He is a legendary player without a legend, probably the most muted of the

Sisler showing how easy it is.

.400 hitters. Cobb, Hornsby, Williams—three of Sisler's fellow members of baseball's most elite batting club—batted .400 and left behind almost as many stories as base hits. Four-hundred hitter Joe Jackson is recalled for his "perfect swing," his "Shoeless Joe" nickname, his illiteracy, and, ultimately, for having kept bad company. Four-hundred hitters Harry Heilmann and Bill Terry left behind a few tales based on their personalities—Harry for his joie de vivre (he once drove his sports car down the steps into a speakeasy), Bill for his dourness and a crack that backfired notoriously ("Is Brooklyn still in the league?"). There is hardly a George Sisler story or quote in the cabinet file, only the sworn-to memories of his flawlessness at bat and afield. Nevertheless, this paragon of ballplaying

perfection came to the major leagues in a roar of controversy.

Sisler was born in Manchester, Ohio, on March 24, 1893. When he was seventeen years old and playing semipro ball, he signed a contract with the Akron, Ohio, club in the Ohio–Pennsylvania League. Akron was then a farm team of the Columbus club in the American Association, an independently owned entity.

When Sisler's father heard about the contract he immediately took steps to have it voided. The elder Sisler understood something about baseball contracts that his more trusting son did not—that those documents contained an insidious provision known as the reserve clause. This clause, which was not removed from contracts until the coming of the free-agency era in the 1970s, bound the player to the signing club until the club decided, by one means or another, to end the relationship.

The case was brought before the National Commission, the three-man ruling council that was the game's adjudicating body before the creation of a commissioner's office. Sisler, who had not played a game of professional ball, was declared a free agent. The National Commission, however, did recommend that George give the Pittsburgh Pirates, who had bought his contract from Columbus, preference if and when he returned to organized ball.

Sisler enrolled at the University of Michigan at Ann Arbor to study mechanical engineering. Inevitably, he played on the baseball team. At that time he fancied himself a pitcher, and soon the young left-hander was making a reputation for himself as one of the outstanding college players of his time. The information was not long in reaching the ears of Branch Rickey, then manager of the St. Louis Browns. Rickey journeyed to Ann Arbor and saw not only a good young southpaw but also a sharp hitter and gifted all-around ballplayer.

By the time he graduated from college, Sisler's baseball abilities were known to every big-league club. Mysteriously, however, only the Pirates seemed interested. By dint of a gentleman's agreement among all the owners, the old, voided contract Sisler had signed was being honored by major-league baseball. Rather than commit the slightest offense against their hallowed reserve clause, the owners were recognizing a contract that their own ruling body had voided.

Branch Rickey, however, refused to enter into this collusion. Always the maver-

ick, Rickey saw to it that the Browns signed Sisler. At this, the Pittsburgh owner, Barney Dreyfus, hit the ceiling, and probably the roof, too. The draconic machinery of baseball's imperial jurisprudence went so far as to suspend Sisler while the question was being investigated. Rickey, determined not to lose his prize, made some not-so-veiled threats about civil law versus baseball law, and the National Commission finally ruled on behalf of the Browns.

Like Babe Ruth a year earlier, Sisler entered the American League in 1915 as a left-handed pitcher with an enchanting bat. Ruth rose quickly to pitching stardom with the Red Sox before being converted to the outfield; Sisler broke in simultaneously as a pitcher, first baseman, and outfielder. (He was coming to the bigs directly off the Ann Arbor campus, with no minor-league experience for the Browns to use as direction.)

Sisler pitched in 15 games and ran a 4–4 record. One of those victories was a 2–1 win over his idol Walter Johnson, an experience George never forgot. The rookie was so emotionally drained by the result, he recalled, that he almost apologized to Johnson after the game.

Overall, the rookie got into 81 games and batted .285. A year later he was the regular first baseman, batting .305 in his first full season. The year after that, he began his lethal machine-gunning of American League pitching.

In 1917 Sisler batted .353, second in the league to Ty Cobb's .383. The Brownie first baseman must have been one eye-catching young ballplayer, for the following is excerpted from an article published in the spring of 1918:

For many years baseball versifiers have derived rich solace from a treatment of the theme "Another Cobb." They have taken the stand that the comparison of a youthful player with the peerless Georgian was the height of absurdity. We know that Cobb has long reigned without equal. We will go further and say that since baseball began he has never had an equal. But a player already wears a major-league uniform who seems destined to fill Cobb's shoes if anyone can. This player has dazzling ability of the Cobbesque type, he is just as fast, showy, and sensational, very nearly if not quite as good a natural hitter, as fast in speed of foot, an even better fielder, and gifted with a versatility which Cobb himself might envy.

This was young George Sisler they were talking about, with just a little under three years' big-league experience and already being bracketed with the prince of all baseball players.

In 1918 and 1919 Sisler maintained his high level of excellence, batting .341 and .352, respectively. Then, in 1920, he erupted into Cobb's rarefied realm and became the greatest player Branch Rickey had ever seen. This was the year that Sisler joined the lions of baseball, batting .407 and racking up his record 257 hits. It was the dawn of the lively ball era, and batting averages jumped accordingly, but none jumped as high as Sisler's, and the Browns' first baseman had his first batting title.

A .400 hitter is the rarest of ballplayers and immediately becomes a national treasure. Fans read that the new hero's personality was "one in a thousand," that he was "one of the most likable fellows imaginable . . . clean, pleasant natured and tireless in his work . . ." He was "highly educated, well informed on all

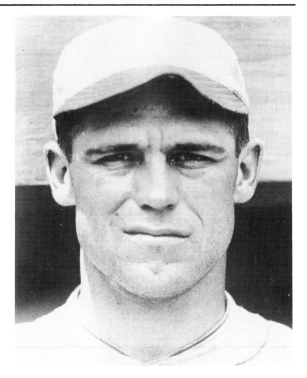

The eyes of a .400 hitter.

subjects . . . able to maintain his end of the conversation with other college-bred men and men of affairs." A visit to his home "shows the highest-grade magazines, technical books, and the classics predominating on his bookshelves." He was "an exceptionally good billiard player, a very fair golfer, and a scientific boxer of no mean ability . . . and a bridge whist player of real skill." It was even duly noted that the newest .400 hitter was "one of the most careful drivers in the city, and has a well-earned reputation of skillfully guiding his big touring car through the mazes of traffic congestion."

In other words, bat .400 in the United States of America and the klieg lights go on and your every burp is made to grand acoustical effect.

Sisler had outhit Ty Cobb, and in 1920

this was a rare feat indeed: Tyrus had taken batting titles in 12 of the previous 13 years.

No player has ever obsessed his colleagues the way Cobb did. If they could not always articulate the psychosis that drove Cobb, the demon that helped galvanize his already formidable natural gifts, then they were sensitive to something that was frighteningly unique, something spectacularly intolerant of all opposition. Among the foremost of Cobb's auditors was George Sisler.

"While never predicting anything for myself," Sisler wrote in March 1921, "I have indulged in daydreams that some time I might match wits with Ty Cobb in a batting duel for the league supremacy, that would not find me second best. This ambition of mine is no secret. For many years there has not been a batter in the league who would not have given his eye teeth to beat out Ty Cobb, although most of them realized the utter hopelessness of the undertaking."

This is like a young heavyweight challenger restless to share the ring with the aging champion. It was true that Sisler had won the title in 1920, but the competitor in him noted wistfully that an injury had hobbled Cobb and held him to a .334 batting average. Sisler hoped "that next season Ty may have a good year, free from injury, and I can assure everyone interested that I shall do my best to outhit him." Four hundred or not, it was

Sisler was with the Washington Senators briefly in 1928. Here he is *(left)* with manager Bucky Harris.

as though before he could cross the Rubicon to his own greatness, Sisler had to best Cobb, swordpoint to swordpoint.

In 1921, Cobb bested Sisler, .389 to .371, but neither won the battle title; Cobb's Detroit teammate Harry Heilmann did, with a .394 average.

A year later, however, in 1922, Cobb turned in one of his greatest seasons, batting .401, and as though this was what he had been waiting for, Sisler blazed away all summer long on white-hot cylinders and ran away from the man who was the universal symbol of batting greatness, turning in a .420 average. It was also, by an eyelash, a record-shattering performance, for Sisler's .420 was higher than the .420 Cobb had turned in in 1911—.4197 to .4196.

That Cobb was Sisler's fixation was further demonstrated in an interview he gave during the 1922 season. When asked what his chief ambitions were, Sisler answered that after playing on a pennant winner his next ambition was "to hang up a higher batting average than Ty Cobb was able to do." He was talking about bettering .4196. This soft-spoken Brownie first baseman evidently had a white-hot pilot burning inside him. (It should be noted that Cobb's average was then the all-time American League high. Years later, however, a review of the box scores of 1901 credited Nap Lajoie with enough overlooked hits to give him an average of .422, which remains the league record. The highest batting mark in the twentieth century is Rogers Hornsby's .424 in 1924.)

A three-year batting average of .400, topped by a colossal .420—and at the age of thirty Sisler was perhaps not yet at his peak. Also, playing at a time when the pitchers were struggling to adjust to the lively ball and lesser hitters than Sisler would be banging away to stratospheric batting averages, the Browns first baseman, it seemed, was at the point of setting even higher standards.

Then, late in January 1923, Sisler suffered an attack of influenza. This led to a sinus infection that brought on a case of double vision. The condition persisted, forcing Sisler to sit out the entire 1923 season.

Though not fully recovered, he returned as playing manager of the Browns in 1924. Yankee pitcher Bob Shawkey recalled how it was:

> When he came back, we soon learned something. And this shows you how mean it was in those days. When he was up at the plate, he could watch you for only so long, and then he'd have to look down to get his eyes focused again. So we'd keep him waiting up there until he'd have to look down, and then pitch. He was never the same hitter again after that.

The man who had an eight-year major-league batting average of .361, who just two years previous had batted .420, hit just .305 in 1924. A year later he came back with a .345 average and 224 hits, but this hardly elated him. "That wasn't hitting," Sisler said.

"He wasn't being a smart aleck about it either," Shawkey said. "Remember, he was down 75 points from his best average. He was looking to hit .400 every year, and if not for his illness he might have done it, too. That's how good he was."

A year later Sisler fell to .290, barely respectable in a league that batted a collective .281.

Resigning as manager in 1927, Sisler batted .327, for him another discouraging

Sisler *(left)* and Rogers Hornsby, when both were with the Boston Braves in 1928.

figure. That December he was sold to the Washington Senators for $25,000. The Senators kept him only until the end of May, then waived him out of the league to the Boston Braves, managed now by his old St. Louis rival Rogers Hornsby. The thirty-five-year-old Sisler batted .340 his first time around the National League, helping Hornsby, who led the league with a robust .387, decorate a dismal seventh-place club.

Swinging on memory, Sisler still had enough left to bat .326 in 1929, rapping out 205 hits, the sixth time he had cleared the 200 barrier. In his final year, the veteran batted .309, again a respectable figure, except that the league overall batted .303 in the most hit-happy season in major-league history. Sisler was released af-

ter the season, his big-league career over.

Despite his "weak" hitting at the close of his career, the accomplishments of his glory years still left Sisler with a lifetime batting average of .340 and a total of 2,812 hits.

For those incorrigible baseball romantics—and there are many—who like to speculate about "what if," perhaps the most intriguing reverie is, What if George Sisler had not suffered the illness that effectively divided his career between unparalleled glitter and mere respectability? Chances are that Sisler would have left behind batting averages of such sublime height that not even Gehrig could have moved him aside as the greatest first baseman of all time.

Jim Bottomley: they called him "Sunny Jim."

JIM BOTTOMLEY

They called him "Sunny Jim," and he was all of that. Always smiling and friendly and easy-going."

That was one of his Cardinal teammates, Les Bell, talking, remembering James Leroy Bottomley some 50 years later. "What a fine gentleman he was," Bell said, "and a great ballplayer. He could do it all."

Sunny Jim did it all for the St. Louis Cardinals right through the 1920s, from 1922 to 1932, when he was traded to Cincinnati. He came to the big leagues in 1922, got into 37 games for the Cardinals as a twenty-two-year-old first baseman, and batted .325. A year later he drilled National League pitching for a .371 average, second best in the league to teammate Rogers Hornsby's .384. It was Sunny Jim's highest batting average, with a .367 mark in 1925 his next best.

Through nine consecutive full seasons, from 1923 through 1931, Bottomley batted under .300 just once—.299 in 1926. Along with his solid batting averages, Sunny Jim was also a consistently high run pro-

ducer. From 1924 through 1929 he drove in over 100 runs per season, leading the league with 120 in 1926 and 136 in 1928, the same year he led with 31 home runs and 20 triples. He also was tops in doubles in 1925 and 1926, with 44 and 40, respectively, and in hits in 1925 with 227. In 1931 he finished third in the closest batting race in National League history, batting .3482 to Bill Terry's .3486 and leader Chick Hafey's .3489.

"Coming that close was almost as good as winning," Bottomley said later, and then with a loud laugh added, "I said *almost.*"

Sunny Jim helped the Cardinals to four pennants, in 1926, 1928, 1930, and 1931. He was one of the heroes in the Cardinals' upset victory over the Yankees in the 1926 World Series, collecting 10 hits in the seven-game championship.

Bottomley came in with the new century, born on April 23, 1900, in Oglesby, Illinois. As a child, he moved with his family to Nokomis, a coal-mining town in the central part of the state. At the age of

A bit of action from the 1930 World Series. Bottomley is out at first base, with Jimmie Foxx having just made the putout.

sixteen he quit school and went to work for the mines, not underground but rather as a blacksmith's apprentice. In mastering that trade he developed muscles that contemporaries described as being "like cords of steel." He soon began using those muscles to lambaste baseballs for a semipro team.

In a game in 1919, the young man exploded with two home runs and three triples, an outburst that caught the attention of the St. Louis Cardinals. The Car-

Jim Bottomley.

dinals signed him to a contract, and his upward progress was rapid: After less than three years in the minor leagues he was brought up late in the 1922 season and thereafter never looked back.

Sunny Jim was an immediate hit, all the way around. Along with his resounding batting he endeared himself to St. Louis fans with his engaging strut and swagger, wearing his cap turned at a jaunty angle, flashing a friendly smile. But Jim also drew himself a reputation in National League dugouts as something of a rube when, as a rookie, he hefted sever-

al long, lightweight, thin-handled bats and asked who was "the guy named Fungo" who used them. The bench jockeys laid that one on him for several years.

He was a direct, uncomplicated man who seemed never to have strayed far from the basics. One evening he was sitting in a hotel lobby lamenting over a slight batting slump.

"I just ain't hitting," Jim said to a sympathetic sportswriter.

"Maybe it's a problem with your eyes," the writer said.

"No, it's not that. Listen, I can put a

Sunny Jim with the Cincinnati Reds in 1935.

newspaper on the floor between my feet, stand up straight, and read the paper."

"Maybe it's your back. A lot of problems start there."

"My back's fine," Jim said.

"Maybe it's indigestion," the writer said. "You fellows are always eating soft-shelled crabs or green cucumbers or some such things."

"My stomach was never better."

Losing patience, the writer asked, "Then what in blazes is the matter with you?"

"I'll tell you what the matter is," Jim said. "I ain't hitting. That's what the matter is."

But Sunny Jim was certainly hitting on the afternoon of September 16, 1924, at Brooklyn's Ebbets Field. It was his greatest day on a ball field, and perhaps the single greatest game that any hitter has ever had, as he set a record that has withstood the long balls and line drives of more than six decades.

In the top of the first inning, Brooklyn starter Rube Ehrhardt loaded the bases with none out and clean-up man Bottomley stepping in. Sunny Jim began his day's work by singling in the game's first two runs.

In the second inning, with Bonnie Hollingsworth on the mound for the Dodgers, Bottomley doubled across another run.

In the top of the fourth inning, against a third Dodger pitcher, Art Decatur, the Cardinals put on another charge. With men on second and third, Dodger manager Wilbert Robinson ordered Hornsby walked to load the bases, choosing to face Bottomley instead—a reasonable move in light of Hornsby's .424 batting average that year. Bottomley, however, made hash of the strategy by driving one over the right-field fence for a grand slammer, giving him seven runs batted in.

In the top of the sixth inning, with Decatur still on the mound, Sunny Jim came to the plate with a man on first and rocketed another shot over the fence, making it nine runs batted in for the day (the score was now 13–1).

It was an impressive performance, and adding some spice to it was the intriguing fact that Bottomley was now just two shy of tying the record for runs batted in for a single game. (The record was held by Wilbert Robinson, achieved when Robbie, then · a member of the old Baltimore Orioles, had collected seven hits in a game on June 10, 1892, and had driven in 11 runs; never a robust hitter, Robinson was understandably proud of the achievement. But now, sitting on the bench and watching the red-hot Bottomley closing in on his RBI record, the portly Dodger skipper was beginning to squirm.)

In the top of the seventh, a fourth Dodger pitcher, Tex Wilson, was on the hill when Bottomley came up with two men in scoring position. Jim singled them home and tied the record.

In the top of the ninth, Hornsby tripled against Jim Roberts and Sunny Jim singled him in to establish a new record and complete a 6-for-6 afternoon's work. (Jim had another 6-for-6 day on August 5, 1931.) The final score was 17–3, with Bottomley driving in 12 runs.

Bottomley was traded to Cincinnati after the 1932 season. No longer a .300 hitter, he put in some respectable years with the Reds and then petered out with the St. Louis Browns in 1937, retiring with a .310 lifetime batting average.

Sunny Jim died on December 11, 1959, after suffering a heart attack while sitting in his car in a St. Louis parking lot.

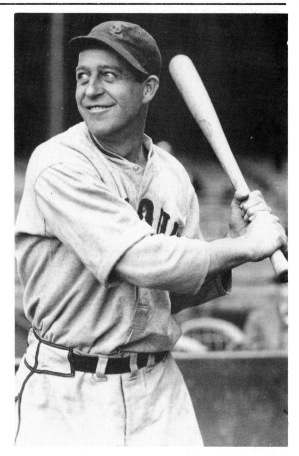

With the St. Louis Browns. He finished his big-league career with them in 1937.

Gehrig missing a high one during spring training at St. Petersburg in 1927.

LOU GEHRIG

"Lou was the kind of boy if you had a son he's the kind of person you'd like your son to be." That was Gehrig's Yankee teammate Sam Jones talking.

"Louie was always a good boy." That was his mother.

"There was absolutely no reason to dislike him, and nobody did." Fred Lieb, sportswriter.

"I had him for over eight years and he never gave me a moment's trouble. I guess you might say he was kind of my favorite." Yankee manager Joe McCarthy.

"I would not have traded two minutes of the joy and the grief with that man for two decades of anything with another." His widow.

Admired, loved, respected, revered. He was perfect in whatever role he assumed: son, husband, teammate, Yankee first baseman. He was strong, heroic, modest, with manly good looks and a dimpled smile.

Few baseball players have ever symbolized so much. His early death has made him the benchmark for sports

tragedy, while his consecutive-game streak has come to stand for endurance and dedication, a sort of stolid and magnificent fidelity to one's responsibilities, through pain, injury, and illness. He never complained, of course, not once, not ever, not about anything, and in this probably lay more the compulsion of the stoic than the grimness of "the silent hero." Even in his celebrated farewell address at Yankee Stadium on July 4, 1939, he conceded that while he "may have been given a bad break" (some bad break: a pitiless, creeping death from amyotrophic lateral sclerosis, a disease that strangles the muscles one at a time), he still considered himself "to be the luckiest man on the face of the earth." He died, two years after diagnosis, quietly and with grace, keeping, as ever, his thoughts to himself.

To maintain unblemished perfection in all quarters and to all sides for so many years is nearly unheard of; it calls for uncommon tolerance and devotion (like playing 2,130 consecutive baseball

Gehrig at Columbia University in 1922.

games across 14 years). Perfection must cause severe frustration at times, and because Gehrig seemed devoid of ego or temperament, there was only one way for him to vent whatever may have been repressed by a lifetime of perceived faultlessness: hitting a baseball.

The stories are common to all power hitters, those tales of how hard they could connect with a ball. In Gehrig's day the stories revolved around Ruth, Foxx, and Lou himself. When it came to distance, the Babe and Jimmie were titans of a special blend. Gehrig was also unique, for not only did he hit a ball "miserably hard" (in the words of one infielder), not only did he hit for distance, but he lashed his shots indiscriminately and with great ferocity to all fields. "The drives he hit to left and left-center were hit just as hard as the ones to right. For power to all fields, there was nobody quite like him," said Bill Dickey, a teammate of Ruth's and a sterling catcher who for years sat under the bat of Ted Williams.

In the special pantheon of left-handed power hitters, Gehrig is alone with Ruth and Williams. These are the left-handed batters who hit not just with spectacular power but for high lifetime averages, too—Williams, .344; Ruth, .342; Gehrig, .340.

Gehrig's year-in, year-out statistics were as inflexibly consistent as his daily appearance at first base. Between 1926 (his second full year) and 1937 (his next-to-last full year) he batted .300 or better every year, eight times over .350, reaching his peak in 1930 with a .379 average.

From 1926 through 1938 he never drove in fewer than 107 runs a season, and eight times he drove in over 140, attaining an American League record of 184 in 1931. That Gehrig was a gargantuan RBI

Gehrig *(left)* and Babe Ruth in 1927.

man is underlined by the following fact: In all of baseball history the 170 mark in runs batted in for a single season has been reached only nine times; on three of those occasions the overachiever was Lou Gehrig. Throughout his career, he averaged nearly one RBI per game (.92) a figure equaled in this century only by Hank Greenberg.

Gehrig's home-run production was similarly consistent. Ten times he hit over 30 in a season and five times over 40, with a peak of 49 in both 1934 and 1936.

Gehrig's other offensive statistics resonate with the same thunderous uniformity: seven times over 40 doubles in a season, eight times over 10 triples, eight times over 200 hits.

This amiable powerhouse played in seven World Series and through those 34 games batted .361 and drove in 34 runs—that consistency again. In the 1928 Series he hit four home runs, drove in nine runs, and batted .545 in a four-game Yankee sweep. In his next Series, in 1932, another Yankee sweep, he hit three home runs, drove in eight runs, and batted .529.

On June 3, 1932, he had his single greatest day, hitting four home runs in a game against the Philadelphia Athletics.

The man most people consider the greatest first baseman of all time was born in New York City on June 19, 1903, just a few months after his future employers, the New York Yankees (then known as the Highlanders), had entered the two-year-old American League. So Lou and the Yankees were a 1903 New York City entry.

Gehrig was the son of German immigrants. By all accounts, the family was dominated by the mother, a humorless woman of frosty disposition and resolute will, whose life centered around her shy, handsome son (her only surviving child of four).

Louie was indeed a "good boy." He was intelligent, obedient, hard-working, and soon he was at Columbia University on an athletic scholarship, studying to be an architect, following his mother's wishes like the dutiful son he had always been.

Mama Gehrig, accustomed to getting her way within her tiny family circle, would have gotten her way again and probably seen her son graduate from college and go on to some desk-bound career, except for one thing: Into her son's robustly muscled body nature had woven some unique qualities, and in this New World of abundant opportunity these were particularly appreciated. Along with the strength were sharply honed reflexes that enabled the young man to

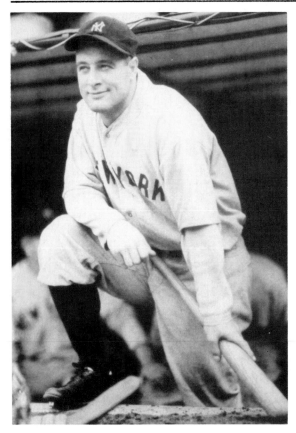

The "Iron Man" in mid-career.

attack a pitched ball with a bat, and the hand-eye coordination that further enabled him to strike that ball with that bat at the very moment the muscles of his shoulders, back, and arms were bunched for the effort. It meant that this boy could knock a baseball 400 or 500 feet. Mama Gehrig might not have known it, but in the United States of America this was a gift that was cherished and amply rewarded.

A talent like Gehrig's is its own natural law, it own justification. It also was the one thing that was stronger and more compelling than the young man's obedience to his mother's wishes. That talent was a roaring, teeming geyser of primal

coordinates, and no obstacle was going to impede it. Here was the quiet, compliant young man's way of defining himself, his own wordless, unemotional mode of self-expression.

Yankee scout Paul Krichell spotted Gehrig playing for Columbia in 1923 and couldn't quite believe what he was seeing. Krichell was one of those Yankee big-game hunters so ubiquitous and so fortuitously stationed in the 1920s and 1930s; they seemed to float like white clouds over a ball field whenever some as-yet-undiscovered talent was making its appearance.

Krichell first saw Gehrig playing for Columbia in a game against Rutgers in New Brunswick, New Jersey. To say that Krichell was impressed would be stating it moderately, for when he returned to the Yankee offices at 42nd Street and Sixth Avenue, he reported to General Manager Ed Barrow that he had discovered another Babe Ruth. If Krichell, a man not given to hyperbole, had announced the discovery of another planet in the heavens it would not have been as startling. Another Ruth? Why, the one they already had was improbable enough, a colossal character and slugger who had knocked baseball completely out of shape and then remolded it in his own image.

For Barrow to be hearing this grandiose announcement was ironic, for it had been he, as manager of the Red Sox a few years before, who had switched Ruth from the mound to the outfield, turning the game's premier left-handed pitcher into its premier slugger. Trusting Krichell's judgment (even if the scout turned out to be only half right it was still quite a find), and knowing that miracles happen only if you believe in them, Barrow told Krichell to have another look and

The infield of the world-champion 1936 New York Yankees. *Left to right:* third baseman Red Rolfe, second baseman Tony Lazzeri, shortstop Frankie Crosetti, first baseman Lou Gehrig.

then, if he still wanted to, sign the boy.

Krichell had his look a few days later, uptown at Columbia's old South Field, and what he saw confirmed his judgment and added to his zeal. Gehrig tied into a pitch and hit one of those nonstop home runs that gets caught in the tailwind of legend and just keeps on riding, borne forever on the wings of history. This one left South Field, shot over 116th Street, and bounced up the steps of the library, as if, as one writer said, "rushing straight for the history books."

The Yankees signed him soon after, giving him a bonus of several thousand dollars, which Lou dutifully turned over to his parents, helping to mollify his mother's moody disapproval of her son's new choice of career. So Gehrig turned professional, relinquishing his Columbia scholarship.

After playing a season and a half for Hartford in the Eastern League, the twenty-two-year-old Gehrig joined the Yankees to stay in 1925, though not yet as a regular. The regular first baseman was Wally Pipp. Pipp, an 11-year veteran, was a solid performer, having twice led the league in home runs. The year before, he had batted .295 and driven in 113 runs.

Obviously not a man easily displaced. Wally, however, was soon to become a permanent adjunct to the legend of Lou Gehrig.

On June 2, Pipp reported to Yankee Stadium with a nagging headache. Manager Miller Huggins told him to take the day off, then told young Gehrig that he was playing. That was June 2, 1925. The next time Gehrig did not play was May 2, 1939. (Pipp reappeared in 1926 as Cincinnati's first baseman, no doubt having taken a vow of silence about his aches and pains.)

Gehrig played in 126 games and batted .295, the lowest he would bat until 1938, his final full season, when he again batted .295. There was something oddly cyclical about his career: It was launched by someone else's minor ailment, it was terminated by his own mortal illness; it began in the shadow of Ruth, ended in the shadow of DiMaggio; and those bracketing .295 batting averages, in themselves symbolizing the return, the end.

By 1927 Gehrig was the game's second-most-devastating hitter, batting fourth to Ruth's third, forcing the opposition to pitch to the great man. They were the most lethal one-two punch ever seen in baseball, and in 1927 they were never better, combining for 107 home runs, 339 runs batted in, 214 extra-base hits, and a batting average of .365 (Lou batted .373, Babe .356).

Gehrig hit 47 home runs that year (only Ruth had ever hit more in a season) and drove in 175 runs, a new major-league record. It was the first of his five RBI titles. In 1930 he drove in 174, in 1931 184, still the American League record. He followed his .373 season in 1927 with an average of .374 in 1928, and in 1930 he

The New York Giants' Mel Ott *(left)* and Gehrig posing during the 1936 World Series.

batted .379, his high-water mark. His lone batting title came in 1934, when he won the Triple Crown with a .363 average, 49 home runs, and 165 runs batted in. In 1936 he again hit 49 home runs, winning his third home-run title. His final year of heavy production was 1937, when he batted .351, hit 37 homers, and drove in 159 runs.

In 1938 he slumped—for Gehrig it was slumping—to .295, with 29 home runs and 114 RBIs. Some people felt that at the age of thirty-five he was slowing down. No one suspected the truth, that the insidious disease that would take his life three years later had begun to atrophy his muscles.

Gehrig swinging away in April 1939, in one of the last games he ever played.

He worked hard in spring training in 1939, hoping to get himself back to his accustomed high standards. But the change in him was painfully discernible. He swung hard but hit softly and had trouble pulling the ball. He ran hard but seemed to get nowhere. He looked, one teammate said, "like a man running through waist-high water."

His teammates kidded him, told him he was getting old. But then the jokes stopped and they merely watched and said nothing. His manager, Joe McCarthy, kept his own counsel. The shrewd and compassionate skipper knew there was more at stake here than the contemplation of benching a star player. There was the streak for one thing, and there was Gehrig's pride. But there were other factors, too. The team, for one. Once the season opened it became apparent that Gehrig could no longer play. He added eight more games to the streak, bringing it to a total of 2,130, but through those eight games he batted just .143, with no extra-base hits and only one run batted in. And then there was another factor, for McCarthy finally the compelling one—Gehrig's physical well-being.

"I was afraid he would get hurt out

Lou Gehrig Appreciation Day at Yankee Stadium on July 4, 1939. Yankee manager Joe McCarthy is at the right.

there," McCarthy said. "I was afraid he'd get hit with a pitch. You see, he wouldn't have been able to get out of the way. He couldn't move fast enough. That's how bad it was."

On the night of May 1, an off day, manager and star met in McCarthy's hotel room in Detroit.

"He asked me how much longer I thought he should stay in," McCarthy said. "He asked me when I thought he should get out. I told him, 'Right now.' He told me he agreed."

The streak ended the next day, on May 2, 1939. As Yankee captain, Gehrig walked to home plate at the start of the game and handed the lineup card to the umpire, a card which for the first time since June 2, 1925, did not include the name of Lou Gehrig. The press box had been informed, and an announcement went out over the PA system that today Lou Gehrig was terminating his consecutive-game streak. The distraught Yankee first baseman received a thunderous ovation as he walked back to the dugout. He tipped his cap, then sat down in a corner of the dugout, alone. On his face, one teammate said, was "an expression of soft, sad confusion."

In June Gehrig went to the Mayo Clinic in Rochester, Minnesota. His illness was by this time so advanced, his condition so deteriorated, that the doctors were able to diagnose it virtually by looking at him. Two years, they told him; two and a half at most.

The doctors were on the money. On June 2, 1941, 16 years to the day that he had replaced Wally Pipp as the New York Yankees' first baseman, Gehrig died at his home in Riverdale, New York, a few weeks short of this thirty-eighth birthday.

Bill Terry.

BILL TERRY

Bill Terry was born on October 30, 1898, in Atlanta, Georgia. He started his career in professional baseball before his seventeenth birthday, as a left-handed pitcher for the Newnan, Georgia, club in the Georgia–Alabama League, in 1915, breaking into eight games and logging a 7–1 record (the same year that George Sisler began his career as a left-handed pitcher for the St. Louis Browns). The sixteen-year-old Terry was a mature youth, serious, reserved, sometimes icily so—already displaying the personality traits that would exasperate New York sportswriters two decades later.

Terry pitched for Shreveport in the Texas League in 1916 and 1917, doing well, though sending up no rockets. He apparently was interesting with a bat in his hand, as he got into around 50 games in the outfield in 1917, hitting just .231.

In 1918 Terry went to work for the Standard Oil Company in Memphis, Tennessee, and was out of organized baseball for four years. His duties at Standard Oil included managing the company baseball team.

Terry was well paid, liked his job, and consequently kept passing up opportunities to return to professional ball because he didn't think he would be bettering himself financially. He let it be known that he would accept nothing less than a major-league contract.

Word of Terry's talents finally reached John McGraw, manager of the New York Giants. To play for the Giants was then the ambition of just about every player in the game (although Babe Ruth's robust glamor was in the process of changing that and turning the Yankees into the team of choice for most youngsters). So when McGraw met with Terry and offered him the opportunity to sign with the Giants, John J. was expecting gasps of excitement. According to the story that has come down through the years, Terry's first response was "For how much?" Only one thing concerned Terry: Would he and his family be better off with Standard Oil in Memphis or the Giants in New York? McGraw evidently gave a satisfactory answer, and Terry signed a contract, reportedly for $5,000 a year, which was good money in those days.

McGraw sent the new man to Toledo in

45

Bill Terry in 1928.

the American Association with instructions to learn to play first base. Terry never needed any instruction in the art of hitting: He batted .336 and .377 at Toledo in 1922 and 1923. The latter average told McGraw that Terry was ready.

When Terry joined the Giants in 1924 the club already had a star first baseman in George Kelly. A .300 hitter, an established 100-RBI man who had already led the league in home runs, and an excellent fielder, Kelly was considered one of the league's top first basemen. With his keen eye for talent, however, McGraw saw Terry as a potentially greater player, and Kelly was soon playing second base and the outfield, and a few years later was traded to Cincinnati. John McGraw was never more correct in his evaluation of a player than he was with Terry: The young man from Memphis was to go on to become the greatest of all the Giants

McGraw had in his 31 years as New York manager.

Terry batted only .239 in his rookie season, but McGraw was not discouraged. Taking over as regular first baseman the following year, Bill responded with a .319 batting average.

After dipping to .289 in 1926, Terry began a string of 10 straight seasons—right on through his final year in 1936—of over .300, closing out his career with a lifetime batting average of .341. That figure is the highest of any left-handed-hitting National Leaguer in the twentieth century, and second only to Rogers Hornsby's .358 among all National League players in this century.

Terry's two biggest years came back to back in 1929 and 1930, when he batted .372 and .401, collecting a total of 480 hits over the two seasons. Granted this was an era of extraordinarily high batting averages—Terry's .372 in 1929 was only fourth best in the league that year, and a season later he was one of six National Leaguers to bat over .370. Nevertheless, along with Hornsby (who did it three times), Terry remains the only National Leaguer to clear .400 in this century.

In 1930 Terry had 254 hits, tying the league record established the year before by Lefty O'Doul. Bill was not a home-run hitter, his high being 28 in 1932, though in April of that year he did hit six in four games. One contemporary writer described him at the plate this way: "Terry is essentially a line-drive hitter. His favorite hit is a sizzling single or two-bagger. Such hits travel with amazing velocity and are difficult to handle. A home run to Terry is merely an accident. He didn't hit the ball any harder, but he hit it at a greater elevation."

Terry had over 200 hits in a season six

Terry *(left)* at the 1933 All-Star Game with Washington's Joe Cronin *(center)* and the Athletics' Jimmie Foxx.

times, and six times—consecutively, from 1927 through 1932—he drove in over 100 runs, something no other player in the heavy-hitting league was able to accomplish.

After his .372 season in 1929, Terry was asked if he was hitting over his head (his previous high had been .326). "Perhaps," he said. "There's always a best. Ty Cobb hit .420 in his greatest season. Why didn't he always hit .420? You can enter that in a contest of foolish questions. Will I always hit .372? I'd like to, but it's a pretty hot pace."

The pace got even hotter the next year, when the National League seemed to go berserk at home plate, compiling a collective batting average of .303. Six teams batted over .300, with the Giants topping everyone at .319, and Terry was king of them all with his .401.

The hitting in the majors was torrid all through that 1930 season, particularly in the National League. (The astronomical batting averages were attributed to an especially lively ball, which was toned down the following year.) Terry displayed a breathtaking consistency all season. On June 1, he was batting .390, with Babe Herman leading at .411, followed by Paul Waner's .402. On July 1, Terry was batting .391, trailing Waner, Chuck Klein, and Lefty O'Doul, who was tops at .401. On August 1, Terry was batting .396, fifth in the league behind Herman, O'Doul and Klein, the last of whom had soared to .411. On September 1, Terry led with .405, 14 points ahead of Klein. At the end it was Terry with .401 to Herman's .393.

The following year, with the ball considerably throttled, Terry was again at the top—almost. In the closest batting-title race in National League history, Ter-

ry lost out to the Cardinals' Chick Hafey, 3489. to .3486. (Hafey's Cardinal teammate Jim Bottomley finished at .3482.)

By 1932 Terry had established himself as far and away the best first baseman in the National League, probably the best the league had ever had. It looked like one of the smoothest and most flawless careers in baseball. There was, however, a noise in the night, a loud, abrasive, and unrelenting problem that had been bringing grief and glory to the New York Giants for three decades, a problem that seemed to have broken off from nature and become a law unto itself. Its name was John J. McGraw.

There was no way that McGraw and Terry could have coexisted harmoniously. McGraw was sarcastic, demanding, dictatorial; Terry was quiet, strong-willed, independent. In the changing world of the 1920s, McGraw was no longer getting away with the tactics he had been using since the turn of the century. Players were no longer sitting passively under the withering verbal abuse. Frankie Frisch, the club's great second baseman, with a gift for sarcasm and a combative nature equal to the old man's, shouted back and finally was traded. Freddie Lindstrom, the club's gifted young third baseman, responded heatedly, and McGraw simmered. Terry, less volatile than the others, maintained a disdainful silence in the face of the manager's tirades. Those tirades grew more vituperative and increasingly irrational. In his late fifties, McGraw had become, in Lindstrom's words, "an embarrassing relic."

One day Terry suddenly answered back, briefly and sharply, then turned and walked away, leaving McGraw fuming. After that, neither of these two proud and stubborn men would speak to one

Terry *(right)* and Giants catcher Gus Mancuso.

another. If McGraw had instructions for his first baseman, they were passed along through a third party. After a while Terry accepted the situation almost with a sense of whimsy, as though indulging the antics of a willful child.

It was McGraw who broke the silence, unexpectedly and most dramatically, on June 3, 1932. The old man had grown increasingly irascible, to the point where club owner Charles Stoneham finally decided to remove him. Removing someone who was both manager and institution called for extreme delicacy in the handling. Part of Stoneham's arrangement with McGraw, it was said, was to allow John J. to choose his successor.

It was perhaps McGraw's finest moment. The episode gives telling insight into the depth of loyalty he felt toward his ball club. Wanting to place his beloved Giants in what he believed were the most capable hands possible, he chose the man whom he could not abide personally but whom he respected professionally.

When he was summoned to McGraw's Polo Grounds office on that afternoon of June 3, 1932, Terry thought it was to be told that he had been traded. Instead, to his astonishment, he heard a weary and subdued John McGraw offer him the job of managing the New York Giants. Terry accepted on the spot.

The club Terry inherited was hovering near last place. A year later he led them to the pennant, the team's first in nine years, with the skipper showing the way with a .322 batting average. The Giants then went on to crown Terry's first full season as manager with a World Series victory over the Washington Senators.

To the writers covering the club, the Giants' leap from a struggling, demoralized sixth-place finish in 1932 to the world

Terry *(left)* greeting Brooklyn manager Max Carey in spring training, 1933.

championship a year later was no miracle—it was the players responding to the stimulus of new, encouraging, cooperative leadership. They credited the new manager. Terry's credo was simply stated: "Any big-league team that hustles will win ball games. Hustling comes from confidence that you can get somewhere. The manager's job is to instil that confidence and keep the fellows pulling together."

To the public and to much of the press Terry was a cold and aloof personality. He answered questions politely and to the point, never saying more than he had to. He was considered humorless. Ironically, it was one of Terry's rare attempts at humor that came back to haunt him.

At a press conference a few months before the 1934 season opened, Terry was asked a question about the Giants' bitter intracity rivals, the Brooklyn Dodgers.

"Is Brooklyn still in the league?" Terry asked jocularly.

This is one of Terry's few recorded attempts at levity, and it came back to choke him like an ill-fitting collar at the end of the season.

The Giants and the Cardinals were deadlocked in first place, each with two final games to play. The Cardinals were playing the Reds, while the Giants were playing the Dodgers in the Polo Grounds. The Dodgers, managed by Casey Stengel, were a hapless sixth-place club, but now they suddenly had a chance to redeem their season and send their fans into the winter with a royal sense of satisfaction. And the Dodger fans were there, storming in from Brooklyn to fill the Polo Grounds with roars and cheers and taunts, the loudest being, "We're still in the league, Mr. Terry!"

The inspired Brooklyn club beat the Giants twice and helped send the Cardinals into the World Series.

At the winter meetings that year, Stengel told Terry that he had considered going into the Giant clubhouse after the final game and commiserating with Terry, then had thought better of it.

"It's a good thing you did," the still-smarting Terry said. "You would have been thrown out on your ass."

In 1936 and 1937, however, Terry led his team back into the World Series, losing each year to the Yankees. The 1936 season proved to be Terry's last as an active player. Aching knees had reduced him to part-time status. He batted .310 in his final year.

Terry managed the Giants for four more years, until 1941, when a third straight second-division finish spelled the end. He was replaced by his longtime teammate Mel Ott.

Terry left behind, along with his .341 lifetime batting average and record as a superb defensive first baseman, a reputation as a first-class manager, generally liked and respected by his players. He also left behind memories of a strong, complex personality. One sportswriter wrote of him in 1938, "Those who hate him really hate him. And those who like him decline to be budged an inch." There are some who said that Terry had on his mind money as much as baseball. In his era this seemed irreverent. Terry's response to the charge was characteristic: "I'm giving this game the best years of my life. I'd make any other business pay for that. Why should baseball, because it's a game, be any different?"

Sixteen-year-old Jimmie Foxx, catcher for the Easton Club, in 1924.

JIMMIE FOXX

Connie Mack, a bit of his New England antecedents still evident in his voice, referred to his great slugger as "Fawks." Sportswriters dubbed him "Double-X." Those impressed with his physique and his aura of impacted strength called him "the Beast." And, without fear of contradiction, everyone said he was the hardest-hitting right-handed batter of his time, maybe of all time; and there were those who maintained that he hit as hard as Ruth—this when the two sluggers were contemporaries in the late 1920s and early 1930s. For some baseball purists, this avowal came as close to heresy as it was possible to come. Nobody ran as swiftly as Ty Cobb, nobody threw as fast as Walter Johnson, nobody hit as hard as Babe Ruth. These were the unchallengeable verities of modern baseball's first quarter century.

The true credo of baseball's keepers of the faith was probably not that anyone couldn't hit as hard as Ruth, but that they *shouldn't* hit as hard as Ruth, for how many deities could one game sustain at a time?

Nevertheless, there was Jimmy, burgeoning year by year under the nimbus of such attestations as these:

"I don't care how far it is, how improbable; when somebody points to a spot and tells you that's where Foxx hit one, believe it."—Ted Lyons, longtime ace right-hander of the Chicago White Sox.

"One day he hit one off the center-field wall so hard that the ball shot all the way back to the infield and Jimmie barely made it sliding into second base."—Doc Cramer, Jimmie's teammate on the Athletics.

"We were watching it for two innings."—Cardinals relief pitcher Jim Lindsey, of a home run Jimmie hit in the 1930 World Series.

"It's a damned lie!"—Red Sox teammate Dusty Cooke, jumping out of the dugout to watch one of Jimmie's belts in Cleveland. (The ball, by some estimates, traveled close to 600 feet.)

Nor did James Emory Foxx do these

things just occasionally. He did them often enough to be voted the American League's Most Valuable Player three times (1932, 1933, 1938); to win a Triple Crown (1933); to set an impressive major-league home-run record (most consecutive years with 30 or more home runs—12, from 1929 through 1940); to hold, with Hank Greenberg, the record for most home runs in a season by a right-handed batter (58, in 1932); to leave behind 534 home runs and a .325 lifetime batting average; to bat .344 in three World Series (1929, 1930, 1931). And so on, through 20 years of one of the most resounding careers in the annals of major-league baseball.

This massively muscled powerhouse was, by all accounts, a quiet and most amiable fellow, one of the best-liked players of his time. He was born in Sudlersville, Maryland, on October 22, 1907, son of a dairy farmer on Maryland's Eastern Shore.

Jimmie began developing his formidable muscles working on his father's farm, milking cows, hauling heavy cans of milk, and performing other general chores. When he found time, he played baseball, well enough to be earning a buck a game playing with semipros when he was fourteen. The boy not only could hit, he could also catch, pitch, and play infield and outfield with equal dexterity. He could also run extremely well, something of which he was always proud and reminded people of later on when he was known primarily for his high and mighty clouting.

Jimmie was playing for the Sudlersville High School team and hitting baseballs harder and farther than high-school boys had a right to do. In the United States of America, you can't do that sort of thing for

Jimmie Foxx in 1927.

very long before someone starts to take notice. In Jimmie's case, the someone was not just anyone.

One morning in May 1925, Jimmie walked down to the mailbox and in it found a penny postcard addressed to him. Written in pencil, it was an invitation to try out for the Easton, Maryland, club in the Eastern Shore League. It was signed by Frank (Home Run) Baker, star slugger of Connie Mack's great Philadelphia Athletics teams that were the class of baseball in the years just prior to the war. Baker, who had earned baseball's most glamorous nickname by hitting two pivotal home runs in the 1911 World Series, was manager of the Easton club.

Jimmie showed the card to his father. Dell Foxx, a former semipro catcher, was pleased. "Let's go," he said.

This Foxx kid must have been the real beans right from the start. Baker wanted to sign him immediately. Jimmie, still in high school, had to promise his father he'd go back and finish in the fall before the old man agreed to let him play pro ball. Thus began the spectacular career of Jimmie Foxx.

Jimmie got into 76 games for Easton— he was a catcher then—and batted .296, with 10 home runs. Not bad, considering he didn't turn seventeen until after the end of the season.

It didn't take long for the noise from Jimmie's bat to reach north to New York and Philadelphia. Both the Yankees and the Athletics expressed interest in the robust, smiling, hard-hitting teenager. Baker, still nurturing old loyalties to Connie Mack, steered Jimmie to the Athletics (otherwise a few years later the heart of the Yankee lineup would have read: Ruth, Gehrig, Foxx).

Connie Mack was immediately enamored of the boy, enough to let Jimmie open the 1925 season with the A's. The seventeen-year-old (by baseball standards a prodigy) got into a few games as a pinch hitter, going 6-for-9. "He made a good impression on everybody," Connie said (.667 batting averages generally do). After that, Jimmie took some seasoning with Providence of the International League, getting into 41 games (still a catcher) and batting .327. In 1926 he was with the A's all season, riding the pine most of the way, catching batting practice, getting into just 26 games, mostly as a pinch hitter, and batting .313.

Mack liked Jimmie's bat, but the A's had a regular catcher, Mickey Cochrane, perhaps the greatest of all time. So another spot would have to be found for the young man.

In 1927, Jimmie broke into 61 games, most of them at first base; he batted .323, hitting three home runs. A year later, at the age of twenty, he began playing regularly, catching a few games but dividing the bulk of his activity between first base and third base. In 118 games he batted .328, hit 13 home runs, and drove

in 79 runs. These were solid credentials, but the impression the youngster made went much, much deeper. In an article published in 1928, one writer stated, "Already the wise men of the sport are predicting that this six-foot, 180-pound youngster is swinging a bat that threatens to cast a shadow over the wonderful achievements of the mighty Babe Ruth."

Now, considering the stature of Ruth in 1928 (the Babe was following his 60-home-run season with one of 54), this was pretty audacious talk about a twenty-one-year-old just completing his first full big-league season; but whoever those "wise men of the sport" were, they proved to be shrewd appraisers of talent. In a few years Foxx would be universally acclaimed as "the right-handed Ruth," as gaudy a baseball accolade as it is possible to receive, then and now.

Three dapper big-leaguers get together in Florida during spring training in 1933. *Left to right:* Brooklyn manager Max Carey, Brooklyn pitcher Rosy Ryan, and Jimmie Foxx.

A brace of Philadelphia sluggers posing together before the start of the 1931 season. Chuck Klein of the Phillies *(left)* and Jimmie Foxx.

"He is a natural player," another writer wrote of Jimmie, "another Ruth." That the comparisons came so early in Foxx's career and did not seem outlandish surely gives some indication of the remarkable power the young man displayed (and he was then still years away from full strength, remember). No doubt there were other youngsters compared to Ruth in those days (there was no better way to impress a readership), and of them we know little or nothing; they were curve-balled into anonymity or modest achievement. Jimmie alone made it close. Apparently there was no one else in the hard-hitting post-Ruth 1930s—not Gehrig or Greenberg or DiMaggio—could rocket a baseball with as much frightening dis-

patch as the Maryland farmboy.

That the young Jimmie Foxx was eminently admirable from all perspectives is reported in this 1928 article: "All of his blows soar high and far. They are mighty ones, clouts that come from arms that swing milk cans during the winter instead of cue sticks and with strength that has not been sapped by late hours and gay parties."

These latter remarks are characteristic; Jimmie's friendly, ingenuous personality seems to have enchanted the writers almost as much as his prodigious power. They couldn't say enough about "the rosy-cheeked kid from the sandy soil of the Eastern Shore of Maryland." The boy "means as great an inspiration to rural young America as he does to baseball. His off-the-diamond days are as clean and as honest as are his efforts in the game of baseball. He likes to talk of his cows and his farm work as much as he does of his love of the game."

This was the portrait of a practical and level-headed young man. Jimmie had saved his money and bought a 200-acre dairy farm near his Sudlersville birthplace. "When I get home after the baseball season," Jimmie said, "I never go any farther than to the railroad station with a truckload of milk."

It was all duly and soberly reported. This was, after all, "the next Ruth"—in democratic America all but a crown-prince designation—and the writers seemed delighted that he was a scrupulously upright, "rosy-cheeked," stainlessly pure slice of genuine Americana.

Jimmie remained in tandem with Ruth. As hard as Gehrig was reputed to hit a ball, Foxx must have hit it harder, for he was always first when comparisons with Ruth were made. When they spoke of

Foxx in spring training in Sarasota, Florida, in March 1936. The catcher is Moe Berg.

Ruth, Foxx was not far behind; when they spoke of Foxx, Ruth was not far ahead. No hitter has ever been as consistently measured against the king of all sluggers. "Ruth takes a prodigious cut at the ball," wrote one analyst of the time, "and follows through with the full momentum of his body. Foxx is distinctly an arm and wrist hitter. He takes a quicker but nearly as trenchant a cut at the ball, and he holds the bat with an iron grip."

By 1932 the sportswriters, who had begun anointing him when he was a mere rookie, were now making it sound as though a royal succession was taking place: "Age has slowed down the ponder-ous Babe, robbed him of something of the driving force which made him the greatest hitter in baseball, impaired a little the matchless batting eye, the uncanny timing, in short, has laid a clutching hand upon his laurel crown and now seems destined to bestow that crown upon another."

There was no question to whom that crown was going—to Foxx, who that season had come within reach of Ruth's record, with 58 home runs, and in addition, had driven in 169 runs and batted .364, putting together the kind of season that could only be described as Ruthian. At that, Jimmie might have left Ruth's record in pieces if not for a quirky desire he announced in spring training. He told his teammates he was going to get more walks this year than last, and he did just that—73 in 1931, 116 in 1932. "If he had been free-swinging that year like he always did," Doc Cramer said, "Ruth's record would have gone out the window."

Foxx followed up his 58-homer season with another spectacular outing in 1933; it was, in fact, a Triple Crown season, built on a bedrock foundation of a .356 batting average, 48 home runs, and 163 runs batted in.

All the early, glowing forecasts were now being stamped paid, with dividends. In 1934 Jimmie followed his Triple Crown sweep with a .334 batting average, 44 home runs, and 130 runs batted in. In 1935 he won the home-run crown with 36, while batting .346 and knocking in 115 runs.

Jimmie Foxx, in person.

After the 1935 season, Connie Mack, struggling to survive in a depressed economy, dealt his bruising slugger to the Boston Red Sox in a deal that involved several lesser players and $150,000, a truckload of money in those mid-Depression years.

Jimmie put in six seasons at Fenway Park, including one of the most explosive of his career. This was in 1938, when he won his second batting title with a .349 average and his third RBI crown with the monstrous total of 175 (the fourth-highest single-season total of RBIs in big-league history) and earned his third MVP award. That he didn't win another Triple Crown was hardly Jimmie's fault: He poled a robust 50 homers, but this was the season that Big Henry Greenberg hit his 58 long ones.

Ironically, a year later Jimmie won his fourth and final home-run crown with a total of 35, driving in 105 runs (he missed 30 games) and batting .360. This was 1939, the year he teamed in the lineup with rookie Ted Williams. "They were quite a twosome in the batting order," one American League infielder recalled. "When Ted came up you saw the right side of the infield take a deep breath; and then came Jimmie, and the left side took a deep breath." For pure ball-scalding, the only tandem to match them was Ruth–Gehrig.

Jimmie's days of maximum thunder, however, were now behind him. In 1940 his numbers were still good—36 home runs, 119 runs batted in, a .297 batting average. A year later he had 19 home runs, 105 RBIs, and a .300 batting average. For a young player on the way up, an exceptional season; for thirty-four-year-old Jimmie Foxx, an ominous sign of erosion. He had hit 519 home runs at this point, making him and Ruth the only men to clear the 500 barrier in long-distance shots.

By this time Jimmie had developed a serious affinity for scotch. "He used to say he could drink 15 of those little bottles of scotch, those miniatures, and not be affected. Of course, nobody can do that and stay healthy, and it got to Jimmie later on." That was Ted Williams, remembering Foxx years later. (Ted also rated Foxx, after DiMaggio, as the greatest player he ever saw.)

Whether it was the whisky dulling his reactions or the passage of time beginning to weigh on those impressive muscles, Jimmie faded quickly. After 30 games in 1942, during which he had just five homers and a .270 batting average, Foxx was waived to the Chicago Cubs. Beset by injuries, he got into 70 games that season, hit a meager three home runs, and batted .205. But the power in a dynamite bat is never quite dead, as Brooklyn right-hander Kirby Higbe found out one afternoon in Chicago's Wrigley Field. Victim of one of Jimmie's three home runs that day, Higbe never forgot it. "It was a line drive that went past my ear," he said. "It sounded like a bee. It ended up in the center-field bleachers."

Jimmie did not play in 1943, broke into a handful of games in 1944, and returned in 1945 to help the Phillies round out their war-depleted roster. At the age of thirty-seven, he played in 89 games (nine of them as a pitcher), batted .268, and hit seven home runs, closing out his career with 534 homers, second only to Ruth. Foxx remained in the second spot for another two decades.

Jimmie's postretirement years were a graph of long, sad decline beset by alcoholism. Frequently close to indigence ("I was born to be broke," he said

Playing out the string with the Chicago Cubs in 1942.

ruefully), his wretched state of affairs never seemed to impinge on his sunny disposition or the natural generosity of his big, unselfish heart. Former teammates and friends from the past always reported the same thing: Jimmie insisted on picking up the tab, no matter how thin his resources.

Jimmie died on July 21, 1967.

Tom Yawkey, Jimmie's Red Sox employer and for many years quiet benefactor when the old slugger was scraping the bottom of the barrel, said just before his own death in 1976, "You know, I never met anybody, or heard of anybody, who didn't like Jimmie Foxx."

Greenberg in 1935.

HANK GREENBERG

Hank Aaron was not baseball's first "Hammerin' Hank." The first one was named Greenberg, and he played for the Detroit Tigers in the 1930s and 1940s, hitting the ball with a pulverizing power that made him the peer of Foxx and Gehrig and DiMaggio, with whom he jousted in titanic home-run and runs-batted-in contests. There were times in those bleak Depression years (when the only thing booming in the country, it seemed, were American League bats) when 50 home runs and 150 runs batted in were not enough to lead the league.

No one ever looked more the slugger at home plate than Big Henry (and big he was: nearly six-feet-four, 215 pounds). He stood up straight, bat held high, a sculpture of poised, deeply concentrated confidence, totally at ease with his ability to mash a baseball.

"I loved to hit," Greenberg said. "For me, there were few satisfactions in life equal to stepping into a baseball and really driving it. A friend of mine who fancied himself an amateur psychologist said I was taking out my aggressions on that baseball. Maybe, but I don't think so. I just loved to hit." Understandably. No one who could hit like Big Henry wouldn't have enjoyed it immensely.

Teammate Charlie Gehringer said of Greenberg: "Hank loved to drive those runs in. If there was a man on first, he'd always say to me, 'Get him over to third, just get him over to third.' Everybody likes to drive in runs, but with Hank it was a passion. I think he got just as big a kick out of driving in a run with a single as he did with a home run."

Despite the weight of his awesome power, Greenberg was far from a natural player, far from the design of such contemporaries as Gehringer or Joe DiMaggio, for whom diamond splendor came as naturally as drawing breath. "Hank was a self-made ballplayer," said Gehringer, who was an established star by the time Greenberg joined the Tigers in 1933. "He made himself a great hitter through hard work and determination. When he first came up, he couldn't hit

Detroit rookie Hank Greenberg in 1933.

that curve ball, but he learned to hang in there."

Greenberg was a New Year's baby, born in New York City on January 1, 1911. Although the Bronx boy excelled in all sports at James Monroe High School—including soccer and his favorite, basketball—he was, by his own account, "a big, awkward, gawky kid who was always stumbling over his own two feet." Nature had imbedded power in his bat, leaving it to Henry to work out the rest for himself. He couldn't run very fast, nor was he quite a Hal Chase with the glove. But he had the desire to be a big leaguer, and the determination, and his saving grace —that explosive bat.

His ambition to break into pro ball had to overcome the skepticism of his friends and then the utterly negative opinion of his favorite team, the New York Giants.

When a well-connected family friend tried to get him into the Polo Grounds for a tryout, the word that came back was No: The Giants had already seen him play at Monroe and didn't think he had a future in baseball. What made this evaluation seem almost definitive was the fact that the Giants, with a large Jewish segment among their fans, were always eagerly searching for Jewish players.

But nothing could discourage Big Henry. He continued going to the ball field at Crotona Park, across the street from his home, and cajoling his friends to pitch to him, shag for him, hit him grounders.

"I guess we sort of humored him," one of the friends recalled years later. "Nobody thought he was going to make it. But we were willing to help him out; he was always a nice kid. What impressed us more than anything else was the belief he had in himself. Lord, was he ever determined!"

Young Henry never questioned this urge, this obsession. It was simply one of those imponderables that made sense unto itself, was its own reason for being. "You never ask yourself why you work so hard at making yourself a ballplayer," he said in later years. "Anyway, you'd better not," he added with a tolerant laugh. "You're liable to get some answers that sound funny."

After graduating from high school, Greenberg spent the summer of 1929 playing sandlot ball in the Bronx, waiting to begin classes at New York University in September. Big Henry's booming home runs weren't long in attracting Yankee scout Paul Krichell, the man who a few years earlier had signed Lou Gehrig.

Krichell and the Yankees were so impressed with Greenberg that they offered him a bonus of $10,000 to sign, a mean-

Former Brooklyn Dodger slugger Babe Herman *(left)* and Greenberg in 1937.

The Detroit Tiger infield in 1934 and 1935. *Left to right:* first baseman Hank Greenberg, second baseman Charlie Gehringer, shortstop Billy Rogell, third baseman Marv Owen.

Detroit's "G-Men." *Left to right:* Goose Goslin, Hank Greenberg, Charlie Gehringer.

ingful amount of money in those days. The prudent youngster politely turned it down. His reason was simple: Gehrig. Henry was a first baseman and so was Gehrig, then just twenty-six years old and obviously the Yankee first baseman for at least the next decade.

Three other clubs were interested— Pittsburgh, Washington, and Detroit. Greenberg chose the Tigers, signed for a $9,000 bonus, and in 1930 began his professional career.

He played a few games with Hartford in the Eastern League but spent the bulk of the season with the Raleigh club of the Piedmont League, batting .314 and hitting 19 home runs. The following year was spent with the Evansville, Indiana, club in the Illinois–Indiana–Iowa League (the Three-Eye League, in baseball parlance), batting .318 with 15 homers.

In 1932 Greenberg showed he was ready for the big time. He played with Beaumont in the Texas League and was voted Most Valuable Player, on the strength of 39 home runs and 131 runs batted in. A year later he was Detroit's regular first baseman, breaking in with a .301 batting average, a modest 12 home runs, and 87 runs batted in.

Hank had joined a club that was about to come together and take two straight pennants, a team highlighted by Detroit's hard-hitting "G-Men"—Gehringer, Goose Goslin, and Greenberg.

In 1934 the Tigers won their first pennant since 1909, and Big Henry emerged as a full-fledged star, peer of the reigning first-base titans Gehrig and Foxx. The young Tiger slugger batted .339, hit 26 homers, drove in 139 runs, collected 201 hits, and led the league with 63 doubles, the third-highest single-season total in major-league history.

A year later, helping the Tigers to another pennant, Greenberg earned himself the American League's Most Valuable Player award by batting .328, getting 203 hits, and leading the league with 36 home runs and 170 runs batted in.

The following year Greenberg suffered a broken wrist early in the season and was limited to just 12 games. In 1937, the Tigers insisted he sign a $1-a-year con-

Big Henry.

tract and demonstrate in spring training that he was fit to play before they would offer him a new contract. Having no choice, Hank signed.

Greenberg was not only fit to play, he went on to have what he felt was his greatest season, batting .337, hitting 40 homers, and driving in an incredible 183 runs. It was those 183 RBIs that bronzed this season in Hank's mind (this was, remember, the man who had the RBI taste on his palate every time he went to the plate). His RBI total was Herculean, but it fell achingly short by one run of tying Lou Gehrig's American League record, set in 1931. (The major-league high of 190 was established by the Cubs' Hack Wilson in 1930.)

A year later, in 1938, Greenberg put on one of the most thunderous home-run charges in baseball history. The big Detroit slugger, now one of the most fearsome hitters in baseball, stirred the imaginations of baseball fans by making a steady and emphatic march up the slopes of that particular baseball Olympus on which lay Ruth's one-year glamor record of 60 home runs. Along the way, Big Henry set a new record by hitting two home runs in a game 11 times, four of them in September, when the heat was really on.

As the season went into the long shadows, Hank had 58 homers, with five games to go. The games melted off until it was the last day, with the Tigers scheduled for a windup doubleheader against the Indians. In the first game Hank and his teammates had the misfortune of running up against a young Bob Feller at his blazing peak. With newsreel cameras cranked up to record Greenberg's long shots, they got instead Feller setting a new one-game strikeout record when he

fanned 18 Tigers, two of them Big Henry, who doubled once in four at bats. In the second game, called after six innings because of darkness, Hank got three singles, a good day's work, but not what the newsreels were looking for. So Greenberg remains tied with Jimmie Foxx at 58 apiece for most home runs in a season by a right-handed batter.

Ever gracious, Greenberg maintained that not breaking the home-run record never troubled him, because, as he said, "It properly belonged to Babe, the greatest home-run hitter and ballplayer that ever lived." Those 183 RBIs in 1937, however, did nag at him a bit, because "runs batted in were my obsession," not home runs.

In 1939 Hank turned in an average of .312, with 33 home runs and 112 runs batted in—and was asked to take a $5,000 cut in his $40,000 salary (he was the game's highest-paid player). Those were the days when management possessed all the leverage and was not circumspect in exercising it, blithely sowing the seeds of what after the war was to become the Major League Players Association.

In order to avoid the pay cut, Greenberg had to agree to shift from first base to left field, opening up the bag for teammate Rudy York, a heavy hitter who was a defensive liability everywhere but first.

Playing left field in 1940, Greenberg turned in another year of fierce and consistent slugging, batting .340 (his top average), and leading the league with 41 home runs and 150 runs batted in, taking his team into the World Series, in which he collected 10 hits and batted .357 in a losing cause. His big year earned him his second Most Valuable Player award.

At that point, at the age of twenty-nine, with years of powerful hitting still ahead of him, Greenberg's career came to a halt because of the war. Along with his most luminous contemporaries, DiMaggio, Feller, and Williams, Greenberg's career exists with a significant gap in it. Big Henry, in fact, missed more than any of them. After playing 19 games in the 1941 season, he entered the army on May 7, only the second big-leaguer to leave for military service (the Phillies' Hugh Mulcahy was the first). Greenberg would not return until midway through the 1945 season. (Feller left after 1941, while Williams and DiMaggio played through the 1942 season.)

Unlike many big-leaguers who spent much of their service time entertaining the troops by playing baseball, Big Henry put in some rough time. Rising to the rank of captain in the Army Air Corps, he spent 11 months in war zones in China and India, taking part in the first land-based bombing of Japan in 1944.

Greenberg was mustered out of the service in the summer of 1945 and rejoined the Tigers on July 1. Put right into the lineup (the Tigers were involved in a pennant race), and "playing from memory," Hank hit a home run in his first game and then settled into the heat of a pennant chase.

"It was the strangest thing," he said. "I'd spent years away, in some of the most exotic places in the world, flying over the Himalayan Mountains, dropping bombs on Japan. Hardly saw a bat and ball the whole time. Then suddenly I'm back, right in the middle of a blistering pennant race, with barely time to draw a breath. Talk about getting adjusted to civilian life in a hurry!"

The race went down to the final day of the season. The Tigers needed a win to clinch. They were playing the Browns in St. Louis. It was the top of the ninth inning, the Browns leading 3–2. The Tigers loaded the bases with one out and Greenberg coming to bat. The big man nailed one, dispatching it just fair into the left-field stands for the most resounding home run of his career. Circling the bases, he couldn't help thinking that a

Sergeant Hank Greenberg in 1942.

few months earlier he was in India, wondering when the war would end, and now here he was, trotting home on a grand slam that would win a pennant for the Tigers and send him into his fourth World Series. "I wasn't sure if I was awake or dreaming," he said.

In his half season, despite the rust on his bat, Hank hit .311, had 13 homers, and drove in 60 runs.

The following season his batting average dropped to .277, but the thunder was still there as he led the American League in home runs for the fourth time, with 44, and runs batted in for the fourth time, with 127.

On January 8, 1947, Greenberg was stunned to learn that he had been waived out of the American League and sold to the Pittsburgh Pirates. Shocked and hurt, he decided to retire. The Pirates, however, prevailed upon him to play one more year, sugaring their plea with a salary of $100,000, which made Big Henry the first ballplayer to earn six figures.

Greenberg played that one year for Pittsburgh (at first base again, where he had played for Detroit the year before), and it was a disappointing one. He batted .249, hit 25 home runs, and drove in 74 runs. For the Pirates, however, it was to turn into a good investment, for while he was there Greenberg struck a close (and lasting) friendship with young Ralph Kiner. Through Greenberg's tutelage and his own aptitude, Kiner quickly developed into the greatest home run hitter of his time.

Upon leaving the active ranks, Greenberg moved into the front office. From 1948 through 1957 he was part-owner and general manager of the Cleveland Indians, working for his close friend Bill Veeck. Greenberg later followed Veeck to the Chicago White Sox, as part-owner and vice president, leaving in 1963. It was his final tie with baseball.

The Henry Greenberg page in the record book is impressive. His lifetime batting average is .313. He hit 331 home runs, and although today he is far down on the all-time home-run scroll, when he retired in 1947 he was fifth, led by only Ruth, Foxx, Gehrig, and Ott. In four World Series he batted .318, hitting five home runs and driving in 22 runs in 23 games.

Big Henry shares the top of one impressive list, and this probably would have pleased him more than anything else. The category is RBIs per game for a career. At the head of the list are Lou Gehrig and Hank Greenberg, each of them averaging .92 runs batted in for every game played—almost one per game. For a man who so lovingly savored his every RBI, that is probably the tastiest dish of all.

Toward the end of his life (he died on September 4, 1986), Greenberg was asked which of his accomplishments he was proudest of. To the surprise of his questioner, he did not refer to his 58 home runs in 1938, his 183 runs batted in in 1937, or his famous pennant-winning grand slammer in 1945. He was proudest, he said, of having come up through the ranks as a player to a position of ownership, of having served his country in wartime, and of being remembered as a great Jewish ballplayer. "When I was playing," he said, "I used to resent being singled out as a Jewish ballplayer. I wanted to be known as a great ballplayer, period. . . . Lately, though, I find myself wanting to be remembered not only as a great ballplayer, but even more as a great *Jewish* ballplayer."

Greenberg with the Pirates in 1947, his final big-league season.

Mize in 1939, the year he led the National League in batting.

JOHNNY MIZE

They called him the "Big Cat," and it was most appropriate, more description than nickname. He stood two inches over six feet and weighed around 215 pounds—big but not remarkably so; up close, however, this laconic, quietly watchful man seemed massive. Few batters exuded so poised an air of menace at home plate as Johnny Mize. Few ballplayers ever moved so softly and hit so explosively.

"Whatever he felt inside, stayed inside," said one of his early managers, Ray Blades. "I never saw so composed a ballplayer. They'd throw at his noggin and down he'd go, and then up he'd come, sometimes not even dusting himself off, but just standing there, looking out at the pitcher, bat on his shoulder. Waiting."

He was born John Robert Mize, in Demorest, Georgia, on January 7, 1913. Demorest was so small, Mize recalled, that "I played more basketball than anything else in those days because it was easier to get up a basketball team than a base-ball team. In fact, I played more tennis as a kid than either baseball or basketball because it took even fewer people."

In 1930 the seventeen-year-old Mize was playing on Saturday afternoons for a lumber-company team, earning $10 a game for busting baseballs around the rough-hewn diamonds of northeastern Georgia. In those years no diamond, no matter how bumpy and irregular, in any village or town, no matter how small or remote, was beyond the range of the ubiquitous scouts of the St. Louis Cardinals, then in the midst of building the largest and most productive farm system in organized baseball (at one time it consisted of 50 minor-league teams and over 800 ballplayers, all under the watchful—some said predatory—eye of Branch Rickey).

The thunder in young John Mize's bat finally drew Branch Rickey's brother Frank down to that hot, somnolent corner of northeast Georgia for a look. "He had his look," Mize said, "and offered me a contract."

With the Rochester Red Wings in 1935.

Mize's first full season in professional baseball was 1931, with the Greensboro, North Carolina, club of the Piedmont League. The husky youngster broke in with nine home runs and a .337 batting average. That average was noticeable and would prove typical: It wouldn't be until 1948, 17 years later, that Mize would fall below .300.

The big boy began a slow ascent through the vast Cardinal organization. In those years it was not uncommon for a player to spend five or six years plying his trade in the minor leagues, waiting for a spot to open up on the big club.

In 1932 Mize was with Elmira in the New York–Penn League, delivering a .326 batting average. A year later he split his season between Greensboro and Rochester, batting .360 and .352, respectively, hitting a combined 30 home runs and driving in 136 runs. With Rochester in 1934 and 1935 he batted .339 and .317, losing large parts of each season to leg injuries. The second injury was so severe that one doctor recommended that Mize retire from baseball; but surgery repaired the problem so successfully that Big John was able to join the Cardinals in 1936.

These were the Cardinals of the Gashouse Gang era—Dizzy Dean, Joe Medwick, Pepper Martin, Leo Durocher, and company. They were a noisy, hungry, combative gang of athletes. The new man said little, asserting himself with a crackling bat, impressively enough for the Cardinals to trade their regular first baseman, Ripper Collins, to the Cubs. Mize batted .329 in his rookie season, with 19 home runs and 93 runs batted in. One of the most formidable slugging careers in National League history had begun.

In 1937 Mize established his credentials with definitive impact. He batted .364, hit 25 home runs, and drove in 113 runs, joining with Triple Crown–winning teammate Joe Medwick to form one of the most lethal offensive couplings ever in the National League.

In 1938 Big John batted .337, and a year later he led the league in both batting (.349) and home runs (28). In 1940 his average slipped to .314, but he led the league with 43 home runs and with 137 runs batted in. Mize gives some insight into what it was like to talk contract in those pre–free agent, prearbitration days (particularly what it was like to talk contract with Branch Rickey):

With Cincinnati slugger Hank Sauer *(left)*.

In 1939 I led the league in hitting with .349. Naturally after a year like that you look forward to talking contract. But when I sat down with Rickey, he said, "Well, your home-run production stayed pretty much the same." No mention of my batting average. So the next year I hit 43 home runs, which is still the Cardinal club record, and led the league in runs batted in. But my batting average went down. When I went in to talk contract this time, he said, "Well, your batting average wasn't so good. Would you be willing to take a cut?" I led the league in hitting, then I led the league in home runs and runs batted in, and he wanted to know if I'd take a cut!

Rickey, the team's general manager, had a reputation for selling his star players while they were still in their prime. ("Better a year too soon than a year too late" was his credo.) There were two explanations behind his willingness to do this—the profit margin (Rickey reportedly received 25 percent of the sale price) and the fecundity of the farm system, where the Cardinals had more big-league-caliber ballplayers than they could possibly use. Accordingly, after the 1941 sea-son Mize was sent to the New York Giants for several players and a reported $50,000 in cash.

Mize put in one year with the Giants, batting .305 and leading the league with 110 RBIs, before joining the navy.

In 1942, with the New York Giants.

After missing three prime years during the war, Big John returned in 1946. Limited to 101 games because of a broken hand, Mize still hit 22 homers and drove in 70 runs while batting .337. A year later he soared to 51 home runs and 138 runs batted in, batting .302—his ninth consecutive year over .300. His RBI total led the league, and his 51 homers tied him with Pittsburgh's Ralph Kiner for the home-run crown. They were only the second and third National Leaguers to attain the half-century mark in home runs (Hack Wilson with 56 in 1930 had been the first).

A year later Mize won his fourth home-run title, again tying Kiner, this time with 40. With 125 runs batted in, Johnny had reached the 100 mark in RBIs for the eighth time.

The following year, 1949, before a Yankee–Giant exhibition game during the season, Mize encountered Yankee manager Casey Stengel. Stengel asked the big veteran how he felt.

"All right," Mize said. "But I'm not playing much."

"If you were over here you'd play."

"Well," Mize said, "make the deal."

On August 22, the Yankees did exactly that. Mize was waived out of the National League and sold to the Yankees for $40,000. The Yankees were embroiled in a sizzling pennant race with the Red Sox

Big John *(right)* with Giants teammates Bobby Thomson *(left)* and Willard Marshall.

and wanted the insurance of the big man's bat. At the age of thirty-six Johnny had begun to slow down; nevertheless, he could still hit.

Mize's contribution to the Yankees' tingling pennant victory on the last day of the season was modest, but in the World Series against the Dodgers (his first Series appearance) he was a crucial factor. With the Series tied at one game apiece and the score of game 3 tied 1–1 in the top of the ninth inning, Mize was sent up to pinch hit with the bases loaded and two out. Big John came through, lining a two-run single that sent the Yankees on to a 4–3 victory.

Mize's "second career" with the Yankees, as part-time first baseman and pinch hitter deluxe, was crowned with five pennants and five world championships in five years. In 1950, with about half a season's worth of at bats (274), he hit 25 home runs and drove in 72 runs. In 1951, 1952, and 1953 he led the American League in pinch hits, batting .342 as a pinch hitter over those three seasons. In the 1952 Series he played in five games and hit three home runs.

Mize retired after the 1953 season, leaving behind one of the more impressive hitting careers in baseball history. Despite losing three prime seasons to military service, he still hit 359 home runs. His lifetime batting average is .312 (.320 for his 11 National League seasons). His .562 slugging percentage is eighth on the all-time list, while his .572 National League percentage is second only to Rogers Hornsby's .577 in that league's history.

Big John led the National League at one time or another in every significant offensive department—batting, home runs (four times), triples, doubles, runs scored, runs batted in (three times), total bases (three times), and slugging (three times).

Mize holds the major-league record for hitting three home runs in a game, having accomplished this power feat six times, while his 51 home runs in 1947 remain the long-ball record for left-handed hitters in the National League.

After a long and unaccountable delay, Mize was elected to the Hall of Fame in 1981.

Mize with the Yankees in 1953, his final big-league season, holding the ball with which he collected his 2,000th hit.

Brooklyn Dodgers rookie catcher Gil Hodges in 1947.

GIL HODGES

In 1943, the end of the war seemed remote. Nevertheless, Branch Rickey, recently hired as general manager of the Brooklyn Dodgers, knew that the war must end eventually, and when it did he wanted to be ready; in fact, more than ready—ahead of everyone else. So, while most clubs were concerned with plugging the gaps in their rosters caused by departures to military service and trying to maintain a semblance of major-league efficiency, Rickey was looking ahead to the postwar years.

Brooklyn scouts were scouring the country, with instructions from Rickey to sign any youngster who showed the merest glimmer of natural talent. For Rickey, natural talent meant running speed and a strong throwing arm; these were the God-given abilities that no amount of hard work or skillful instruction could cultivate. Without them, a ballplayer would grow into a liability, no matter how hard he could hit.

The Dodger dragnet brought in quite a few gifted young players, many of them virtually signing their contracts while on their way to military service, seventeen- and eighteen-year-old boys who would stock the Dodger farm system after the war and some of whom would ultimately glitter in Ebbets Field in the 1950s as part of one of the greatest teams in baseball history. Among their numbers were pitcher Carl Erskine, outfielder Duke Snider, and first baseman Gil Hodges.

Born in Princeton, Indiana, on April 4, 1924, Hodges was attending St. Joseph's College in Rensselaer, Indiana, when his diamond skills attracted Dodger scouts.

The strapping youngster was playing third base at the time, but the initial reports filed east to the Dodger office on Montague Street in Brooklyn evaluated him more widely: "Can also give you a good game at shortstop and in the outfield. Has enormous hands and great agility and could probably play first base. Also big enough and strong enough to catch, if such a conversion is desired. Runs extremely well for his size and hits with great power." When Rickey read the report, he said, "It would have been much simpler if they had told us if there was anything the boy *couldn't* do."

Frankly, there was little this abundantly gifted young athlete could not do on a ball field. The Dodgers signed him and hauled him straight to Brooklyn, where Hodges broke into one game at third base before heading for a hitch in the Marine Corps. Gil's major-league debut hardly pulsated with signals of things to come. He came to the plate three times, walked once and struck out twice; in the field he had five chances and muffed two of them. Then it was off to war.

There are three distinct parts to the story of Gil Hodges: his prowess as first baseman of the Brooklyn Dodgers, his skillful managership of the 1969 "Miracle Mets," and his frightening physical

Hodges with the Los Angeles Dodgers in 1958.

strength (like his equally muscular contemporary Ted Kluszewski, Hodges had a gentle nature, for which his fellow ballplayers were grateful).

Tales of almost sinister aura grew around Hodges' strength. There were stories about the young marine stalking the jungles of the South Pacific killing Japanese soldiers with his bare hands. These stories were no doubt apocryphal, but they were enough to cast the soft-spoken Hodges into an almost legendary mold, to the extent that one of his Mets players said that "Gil managed by intimidation." Another Mets player recalled, "He was quiet, gentle, and fair. He was also a very understanding and sympathetic man. All the same, I always had the feeling there was something bottled up in him and God help anyone who forced it out. To tell the truth, I used to tiptoe around him."

When he returned to baseball in 1946,

Hodges in 1951.

The heart of the great Dodger teams of the 1950s. *Left to right:* Carl Furillo, Jackie Robinson, Roy Campanella, Pee Wee Reese, Duke Snider, Preacher Roe, Gil Hodges.

Hodges was converted into a catcher and assigned to the Newport News, Virginia, team in the Piedmont League. He hit eight home runs and batted .278. A year later he made the jump all the way to Brooklyn and spent the 1947 season as a backup catcher, getting into 28 games, hitting one home run, and batting .156. Despite these unimpressive figures, the Dodgers remained high on the young man.

In 1948 Rickey began shaping the team that was going to dominate the National League for the better part of the next decade. With Roy Campanella joining the club, the Dodger catching was settled. Rickey, however, wanted Hodges' right-handed power swing—made to order for Ebbets Field's neighborly left-field stands—in the lineup. Hodges had already demonstrated remarkable versatility. So Jackie Robinson was shifted from first base to second (a more congenial position for him) and Hodges was given the big mitt.

Hodges broke in slowly as a regular,

New York Mets first baseman Gil Hodges in 1963.

batting .249 with just 11 home runs. A year later, however, learning to cope with right-handed curve balls, he batted .285, hit 23 homers, and drove in 115 runs—the first of seven consecutive seasons of over 100 RBIs. He also led National League first basemen in fielding, the first of five times he did that.

By the early 1950s Hodges was a bona fide National League star, having hit 40 home runs in 1951 and regularly driving in over 100 runs a season. On August 31, 1950, he belted his way into the record books by hitting four home runs in a game against the Braves, becoming the first National League player in the twentieth century to hit four homers in a nine-inning game.

On a team of stars (those Dodger squads included Pee Wee Reese, Roy Campanella, Duke Snider, Jackie Robinson, and Carl Furillo) Hodges was ex-traordinarily popular. This was proven not when Gil was smashing any of his 370 lifetime home runs or driving in any of his 1,274 runs; this was a fan devotion that was demonstrated under exceptional conditions, when such devotion is seldom seen—when Hodges was going through one of the worst and most conspicuous slumps of his career.

It happened during the 1952 World Series against the Yankees, when Hodges endured the painful futility of going 0-for-21 in the seven-game Series. As the slump persisted, the cheers of encouragement grew louder. When Hodges opened the 1953 season mired in another long slump, the cheers continued. Veteran baseball men were impressed; they had never seen such a display of affection for a player in duress.

Hodges soon showed the fans that their loyalty and patience had not been misplaced. In 1953 he responded with 31 home runs, 122 runs batted in, and a .302 batting average, and then ripped the ball for a .364 average in the World Series against the Yankees. A year later he put together what was statistically his most resounding charge through the schedule, hitting 42 home runs, driving in 130 runs, and batting .304—all career highs.

Hodges continued hitting the long ball and driving in runs and playing first base with unsurpassed excellence even after the Dodgers left Brooklyn to prospect for gold and pennants in Los Angeles after the 1957 season.

Though his great years were behind him now, Hodges still had enough thump left in his bat to help the club to a pennant in 1959, getting into his seventh and final World Series, against the White Sox, in which he won the fourth game for his team with an eighth-inning home run.

Despite his wretched 0-for-21 record in the 1952 Series, Hodges, who played for the Dodgers in the World Series in 1947, 1949, 1952, 1953, 1955, 1956, and 1959, still batted .267. He was the hero of Brooklyn's seventh-game victory over the Yankees in 1955, driving in both runs in Johnny Podres' memorable 2–0 win.

After four seasons in Los Angeles, Hodges returned to New York when he was selected by the Mets in the expansion draft, a move that was hugely popular in the city. Slowed by injuries now, the thirty-eight-year-old first baseman broke into just 54 games, batting .252. The following May he was dealt to the Washington Senators, who wanted him as manager. When he left the National League, Hodges held the league record for most grand-slam home runs, 14 (his record was later surpassed by Henry Aaron's 16 and Willie McCovey's 18).

No longer an active player, Hodges managed the Senators from 1963 through 1967 and could have continued in the job, but when the Mets received permission to talk to him about managing their perennial tail-enders, Gil once more returned to New York.

After a ninth-place finish in 1968, Hodges and his Mets suddenly turned the

Manager of the Washington Senators.

National League—and New York City—upside down by surging to the most improbable pennant and world championship in baseball history. Mets ace Tom Seaver gave the skipper a large share of the credit. "All season people kept waiting for the bubble to burst," Seaver said. "But Gil wouldn't let it happen. He'd been through too many grueling pennant races. He never let us get too high, he wouldn't let us get too low. He instilled confidence, he made you feel like a winner, he kept you motivated."

A year before this pinnacle achievement, on September 24, 1968, Hodges had suffered a heart attack in Atlanta. Against all odds, he had returned to manage a world-championship team. For several more years he seemed as robust as ever, but then, on April 2, 1972, during the closing days of spring training, Hodges suddenly suffered a massive and fatal heart attack while walking to his motel in West Palm Beach, Florida. It happened two days before what would have been his forty-eighth birthday.

Hodges accepting congratulations in the Mets clubhouse after the 1969 World Series victory over Baltimore.

Ted Kluszewski.

TED KLUSZEWSKI

"Everybody liked Ted Kluszewski," a Cincinnati sportswriter said one night, reminiscing about the former Cincinnati first baseman years after Kluszewski had retired. "He was one of the nicest and most congenial men ever to play big-league baseball. Very gentle and good-natured. And that was one of the most salutary things ever to happen to big-league baseball—that Ted Kluszewski was gentle and good-natured."

The writer was referring, of course, to the enormous strength packed into Kluszewski's six-foot-two-inch, 225-pound body. When a Cincinnati player described Walker Cooper, for a time a teammate on the Reds in the Kluszewski era, as "the strongest man I ever met," someone asked, "What about Kluszewski?" The player thought for a moment, then replied, "I was thinking about ordinary human beings."

How strong was the Cincinnati first baseman? No one was willing to find out. One pitcher, known for his head-hunting propensities on the mound, was asked if he had ever thrown at Big Klu.

"Are you out of your mind?" the pitcher asked. "Suppose I plunk him and he decides to come out there after me? Who's gonna stop him, and what happens when he reaches me?"

Kluszewski's aura of strength was enhanced by his habit of cutting off his uniform sleeves, exposing his intimidating biceps.

"When he leaned over the plate," Dodger pitcher Johnny Podres recalled, "it looked like his hands and forearms were growing out of watermelons."

The reason for the cut-down sleeves, however, was pragmatic rather than tactical, as Kluszewski explained:

When I first came up with the Reds in the late 1940s the uniforms at that particular time were wool flannel, and they never seemed to make an armhole big enough for me. I kept telling the guy who outfitted us to shorten the sleeves because they bothered me. But he didn't, for some reason, and so I took a scissors and did it myself. But it was strictly as a matter of comfort. I guess those big

83

arms hanging out over the plate did look kind of menacing, but that was never my intention. Believe me, I was a big, peaceful guy trying to get a few base hits and make a living.

As far as being "the strongest man in baseball," Kluszewski said:

People sometimes think it's fun to take a poke at a guy who has that kind of reputation. I can remember reading when Joe Louis was heavyweight champion how now and then somebody would walk up to him and take a swing at him, just for the hell of it, because it was Joe Louis. But luckily I never had any problems along those lines. And now that it's all safely in the past, I can let you in on a secret: I wasn't much of a fighter anyway.

Born on September 10, 1924, in Argo, Illinois, Kluszewski seemed to have been molded by nature for football, and this was indeed his first serious sport. He was good enough to win a football scholarship to the University of Indiana. His play in the Big Ten Conference began attracting the attention of pro football teams when he was still just a sophomore, and the big boy was thinking in terms of a career on the gridiron.

At the same time, he was playing for the varsity baseball team, hitting the ball hard and far. It was one of the university groundskeepers who alerted the Cincinnati Reds to the muscular young man. A few scouts came by, listened to the crack of the bat, and signed him to a contract. This was in 1945.

The Reds were impressed enough to start Kluszewski out with their Columbia, South Carolina, team in the South Atlantic League, a fast brand of ball. Ted demonstrated the acuity of their judg-

Kluszewski taking his cuts in spring training, 1953.

With Pittsburgh in 1958.

Kluszewski batted .274 in his rookie year, then followed up with seasons of .309, .307, .259, and .320. After five big-league seasons he was solidly established, though not as a power hitter. His home-run high was 25 in 1950. In 1952 he hit just 16. Over the next four years, however, his home-run totals soared to 40, 49, 47, and 35, accompanied by RBI totals of 108, 141, 113, and 102, and batting averages of .316, .326, .314, and .302. (Also, the power-hitting Klu never fanned more than 40 times a season.)

What accounted for his sudden ascent among the National League's top home-run hitters? The explanation comes from Kluszewski:

> In spite of my size, when I came up I was a spray hitter. During my first few years my home-run totals were very modest, until 1953, when all of a sudden I hit 40. No, I didn't start swinging for the fences. It was the pitchers who forced me into hitting home runs. They found out they couldn't pitch me outside because I'd go with the ball. So they started coming inside. Well, if you adjust correctly you have to pull the ball, and when you pull the ball you just naturally hit more home runs. That's what happened with me.
>
> Another factor in there was the idea of self-preservation for the pitchers. You see, when they were pitching me outside I was hitting a lot of line drives through the box. I must have been getting about a dozen pitchers a year with line drives, and they began thinking about that. I guess they figured they'd rather run the risk of throwing a home-run ball than getting shot off the mound.

Kluszewski's 49 home runs and 141 runs batted in led the league in 1954, as did

ment by leading the league with a .352 batting average. A year later he was with Memphis of the Southern Association and won another batting title, tearing up the league with .377 average. In 1948 he took over first base for the Reds.

Uncertain around the bag at first, Kluszewski took well to the Reds' tutoring, to the point that he set a major-league record for first basemen by leading the league for five consecutive years in fielding, from 1951 through 1955.

But it was with his bat, of course, that Klu made his living. And he didn't do it with finesse, according to Pittsburgh manager Billy Meyer. "He doesn't rely on perfect timing, the way Babe Ruth and a lot of other power hitters did," Meyer said. "He just lets fly and overpowers the ball."

his 192 hits in 1955. The big man was wistful about those 49 home runs. "I never swung for home runs," he said, "until I got to 49. Then I got anxious. I wanted number 50. Not many guys have popped that many in a year. I had about five games to go but couldn't get it. Forty-nine without trying, and then try like hell and nothing. Is there a moral in there somewhere?"

In the spring of 1956, while reaching for a ground ball, Kluszewski felt something go in his back. "It was almost a year and a half before the problem was diagnosed correctly," he said. "I played a full season in 1956, but the pain kept recurring, coming and going. I'd be able to swing the bat great one day, then not be able to move the next. They eventually found out it was a slipped disc."

Surgery could have corrected the problem, but at the cost of just enough mobility to make the difference, as Kluszewski said, "between being a ballplayer and just another guy walking down the street."

He played on, but with great diminishment. In 1957 he got into only 69 games (most of them as a pinch hitter) and a year later was traded to Pittsburgh. He batted .292, but his power had been drained to the point where in 100 games he hit just four home runs.

Late in the 1959 season he was waived out of the league and picked up by the Chicago White Sox, which was the foreground for what Kluszewski called the high point of his career. He had joined a club that was on the way to a pennant, and that fall Big Klu got into his one and only World Series. He made it a memorable one.

In the White Sox's loss to the Dodgers, Kluszewski set a record for a six-game Series with 10 runs batted in. He hit two home runs in the opening game, three overall, and batted .391. It came as a most satisfying dividend to a superb career that was slowly nearing its conclusion.

After another year with the White Sox and one final season with the Los Angeles Angels (as they were then known), Kluszewski retired in 1961. Though impeded by the back injury that had struck him in his prime, he still hit 279 home runs and had a lifetime batting average of .298.

Kluszewski with the Chicago White Sox in 1959, the year he starred in the World Series.

With the Los Angeles Angels in 1961, Big Klu's last year in the big leagues.

Orlando Cepeda.

ORLANDO CEPEDA

Orlando Cepeda was born in Ponce, Puerto Rico, on September 17, 1937. His father, a legend on the island, was considered the greatest ballplayer in Puerto Rican history, indeed, was known as "the Babe Ruth of Puerto Rico." The son proved to be a spark off the same anvil, developing into one of the most feared power hitters of his time.

The boy was just seventeen years old when he was signed by the New York Giants for a $500 bonus. This was in 1955. Orlando was sent to the Salem, Virginia, club in the Appalachian League. There, in the small, segregated town, he tried to live by the advice given to him by a friend just before leaving home: "Pay no mind to injustices, keep your temper in your pocket, remember Jackie Robinson, and go out and hustle." Sound advice, which the boy tried to follow. Still, he found himself wretchedly unhappy in what to him was an alien and unfriendly environment. As the weeks passed, Cepeda, who spoke no English, became increasingly lonely and depressed. (Making it worse was the fact

that his father had died just before the season opened.)

His performance reflected his state of mind: After 26 games he was batting .247, with only one home run. A friend in Puerto Rico, aware of the youngster's unhappiness, wrote to the Giants explaining the situation. The club quickly transferred Cepeda to the Kokomo, Indiana, team in the Missouri–Ohio Valley League. The change in scenery proved congenial, and here a more relaxed Cepeda was able to apply his full concentration to his game; his bat came to life with a rip and a roar.

Cepeda (a third baseman in those days) got into 92 games and batted a thunderous .393; to that league-leading average he added 21 home runs and 91 runs batted in.

The following year he was promoted to St. Cloud, Minnesota, in the Northern League, where his bat continued to smoke. Shifted to first base now, he won another batting crown with a .355 average, and in fact made it a Triple Crown by leading in home runs (26) and runs batted in (112).

Promoted to the Giants' top farm club at Minneapolis in the American Association, Cepeda in 1957 honed his talents for his inevitable promotion to the top, with a .309 batting average, 25 home runs, and 108 runs batted in. When he broke into the big leagues the next year, however, it was not with New York, but San Francisco.

It was in the summer of 1957 that San Franciscans heard the good news—the New York Giants were leaving the city of their origin and relocating in San Francisco. Along with them, the Giants were bringing the man generally regarded as the monarch of all ballplayers, their twenty-six-year-old center fielder Willie Mays.

1958's Rookie of the Year.

Instead of being unconditionally elated at the prospect of having Mays in their midst, many San Franciscans adopted a somewhat independent posture. They would make up their own minds about who their hero would be and not be led on the subject by the Eastern press. They were not novices when it came to ballplaying splendor, particularly in center field; after all, hadn't they watched the great DiMaggio play it for three years?

So, almost perversely, San Francisco fans were looking for a hero they could claim as their own; in Orlando Cepeda they found him. He was brand new, a rookie, and he was genuine. He started hitting and he never stopped. He batted .312, hit 25 home runs, drove in 96 runs, and was voted the National League Rookie of the Year.

It was a smashing debut, a posting of what for most players would have been career-high statistics. But Cepeda would

The big swing of Orlando Cepeda.

top that batting average three times, the home-run total six times, and the RBI total eight times.

Cepeda was one of an unusually large crop of gifted rookies who arrived with the Giants in San Francisco. Along with Cepeda (nicknamed "the Baby Bull" for his powerful physique) were Felipe Alou, Leon Wagner, Willie Kirkland, and Jim Davenport. The best of the lot, however, was the strong, right-handed-hitting young slugger from Ponce, Puerto Rico, more popular in San Francisco even than Mays. Willie, secure in his stardom, described the young first baseman as "the most relaxed first-year man I ever saw. He's strong, he hits to all fields, and he makes all the plays." And, Willie added dryly, "He's annoying every pitcher in the league."

Cepeda was described as quiet, modest, a gentleman. One player who had known him in Puerto Rico, however, confided that the young man had an explosive temper. This suddenly became evident during a game in Pittsburgh when, during a brawl between the Giants and the Pirates, Cepeda grabbed a bat and ran out to intercede. Only a flying tackle by Mays (ever alert on a ball field) prevented the incensed rookie from getting into serious trouble.

When Willie McCovey joined the club late in the 1959 season and broke in with a bat that wouldn't quit, Cepeda was moved to left field. Orlando didn't like it in the outfield, where he was to divide his time with first base for several years before returning full-time to the bag in 1962.

While he may have been uncomfortable in the outfield, Cepeda remained at ease at home plate. In 1959, he followed up his fine rookie season by hitting .317, with 27 home runs and 105 runs batted in.

At bat for the St. Louis Cardinals in 1967, the year he was the National League's Most Valuable Player.

Cepeda *(center)* with Cardinal teammates Tim McCarver *(left)* and Roger Maris.

In 1960, he batted .297, with 24 home runs and 96 RBIs.

In 1961 Cepeda put together an explosive slugging season, the best of his career: a .311 batting average and league-leading figures in home runs (46) and runs batted in (142). He followed this in 1962 with another strong season, batting .306, hitting 35 home runs, and driving in 114 runs. His heavy gunning helped the Giants get into the World Series, though it proved to be a disappointing one for the team (they lost in seven to the Yankees) and for Cepeda personally (he had just three hits and batted .158).

In 1963, Cepeda joined with Mays and McCovey to form the strongest-hitting trio in baseball. Cepeda hit 34 home runs, Mays 38, and McCovey 44, with Orlando batting .316 and driving in 97 runs. A year later the Baby Bull continued his consistent slugging with 31 home runs, 97

runs batted in, and a .304 batting average, making it six out of seven years of over .300, seven straight years of over 95 runs batted in, and four straight seasons with 30 or more home runs.

In 1965, a knee injury incapacitated Cepeda for virtually the entire season (he had just 34 at bats). The injury was not only painful for Orlando, it also led to a strain in his relationship with Giants manager Herman Franks, who seemed to feel that Orlando was taking too long to recuperate.

With Cepeda injured, McCovey played first base all year, and Franks soon became partial to Willie. Accordingly, in May 1966, the Giants made one of the ill-advised trades they were notorious for, sending Cepeda to the St. Louis Cardinals for left-handed pitcher Ray Sadecki. (In the course of a decade the Giants traded, along with Cepeda, the three Alou brothers, George Foster, and

Gaylord Perry, with little to show for it.)

The trade, Cepeda said, "was the greatest thing that has ever happened to me." Cardinals manager Red Schoendienst quickly installed the new man at first base and as cleanup hitter. Cepeda responded by batting .303 for St. Louis.

The following year, the big man helped hammer the Cardinals into the World Series, batting .325, hitting 25 home runs, and leading the league with 111 runs batted in. It earned him the Most Valuable Player award. A year later, the Cardinals again won the pennant, but Cepeda batted just .248, with corresponding drops in homers and RBIs.

In March 1969, Orlando was dealt to the Atlanta Braves for Joe Torre. It was not a good year for Cepeda, who batted .257, with 22 home runs. He came back in 1970, however, and rapped out a standard Cepeda year—.305 batting average, 34 home runs, and 111 RBIs. It proved to be his last .300, 100-RBI season.

With the Boston Red Sox in 1973, his last full season in the big leagues.

Hobbled by injuries, Cepeda suffered through two disappointing seasons. In June 1972 he was traded to the Oakland Athletics, for whom he played in only three games.

Signed as a free agent by the Red Sox in 1973, Cepeda, no longer swift afoot or agile in the field, was Boston's year-long designated hitter. In this capacity he batted .289, hit 20 home runs, and drove in 86 runs. The Red Sox, however, elected to go with younger players, and in 1974 Cepeda was released.

After playing a few months of the 1974 season with the Yucatan club of the Mexican League, Cepeda signed with the Kansas City Royals in early August and took his final voyage through a major-league schedule. It was a dismal conclusion to a splendid career: In 33 games he batted .215 and hit one home run.

For his 17-year major-league career, Orlando Cepeda batted .297 and hit 379 home runs.

With the Atlanta Braves in 1970.

Willie McCovey: "The most feared hitter in the league."

WILLIE McCOVEY

When sportswriters wrote that Willie McCovey was the most feared hitter in the National League, they weren't spouting rhetoric. In fact, their claim was easily documented, particularly in 1969, when Willie set a major-league record by receiving 45 intentional walks. That's a feared hitter all right, and not just in 1969 either, since the Giants' six-foot-four first baseman holds the records for most seasons with 20 or more intentional bases on balls (five) and for most seasons leading the league in that category (four).

There was ample reason for excusing McCovey from swinging in critical situations; he had a dossier that vibrated with the following: Twice he hit two home runs in an inning, on April 12, 1973, and on June 27, 1977; three times he hit three home runs in a game, on September 22, 1963, April 22, 1964, and September 17, 1966; he led the National League in home runs in 1963 with 44, and in back-to-back years (1968 and 1969) led in both home runs and runs batted in, with figures of 36

and 105, and 45 and 126; he led the National League in slugging percentage three straight times, in 1968, 1969, and 1970; he is the National League record holder for home runs by a left-handed hitter, with 521, and for grand slams, with 18; he was the Rookie of the Year in 1959 and the National League's Most Valuable Player in 1969.

Born in Mobile, Alabama, on January 10, 1938, Willie was one of 10 children. "He grew early and often," in the words of a childhood friend, and by the time he was fourteen Willie was playing semipro ball, already demonstrating that swing of ferocious symmetry that was to intimidate National League pitchers for two decades. Willie's cut at home plate was described by some as the purest since Ted Williams'. With that swing, with his gangly height (they called him "Stretch"), pitchers hated to see him standing at the plate. When he swung, he looked as though he was covering everything, in the words of one pitcher, "from the inside

McCovey *(left)* with fellow timbermen Willie Mays *(center)* and Orlando Cepeda.

corner to halfway up the third-base line."

Growing up, Willie idolized Ted Williams and Stan Musial, and he was a Brooklyn Dodger fan. He dreamed of playing in the big leagues, and when he was seven years old the dream was warmed to its very center, for it was then, in 1945, that Jackie Robinson was signed by the Dodgers, breaking the odious color barrier and laying the first paving stone to guide black players into organized ball.

A New York Giants scout was tipped off about Willie, and the result was a bus ticket for the seventeen-year-old boy to the Giants' tryout camp in Melbourne, Florida. This was in the spring of 1955. Willie showed enough to earn himself a $500 bonus and a contract (at $175 per month) with the Sandersville club in the Georgia State League.

The young first baseman did well in his first minor-league season, batting .305, hitting 19 home runs, and driving in an eye-catching 113 runs in 107 games. A year later, playing with the Danville, Virginia, team in the Carolina League, Willie batted .310 with 29 home runs. They were beginning to talk about him now in the Giants organization, and it wasn't just because of those good statistics: It was that swing. For baseball people it was positively hypnotic.

Injuries slowed McCovey at Dallas (in the Texas League) the next year, but in 1958 he turned in a good season with Phoenix, the Giants' top farm club, in the Pacific Coast League, batting .319.

McCovey went to spring training with the Giants in 1959, but with little hopes of making the club, not through any fault of his own. The team's first baseman was a most formidable player—the National League's 1958 Rookie of the Year, Orlan-

Willie McCovey.

do Cepeda. Behind Cepeda was Bill White, a gifted first baseman recently returned from military service.

White was traded to the Cardinals before the season opened, and McCovey was sent back to Phoenix, where he soon presented his employers with a most pleasant dilemma. After 95 games he had hit 29 home runs, driven in 92 runs, and was batting .372. The Giants could no longer keep him down on the farm.

Willie reported to the Giants in San Francisco on July 30 and was immediately inserted into the lineup, with Cepeda being shifted to third base (where he played a few games and then was moved to the outfield). The Giants were playing the Phillies, and the first big-league pitcher Willie faced was no less than Robin Roberts. McCovey crashed through the gate that day as few rookies have ever done, belting two singles and two triples. He was, in fact, only the third National League rookie since 1900 to break in with four hits in his first game (the others were Casey Stengel

with the Dodgers in 1912 and Ed Freed with the Phillies in 1942).

Willie played in 52 games for the Giants in 1959, batting .354 and hitting 13 home runs, and he was so imposing a figure that he was voted Rookie of the Year despite playing just a third of a season.

McCovey, however, did not immediately follow up on his flashy beginning. In 1960 he batted .238 and was even returned to the Pacific Coast League for a few weeks.

Playing primarily against right-handed pitching in 1961 and 1962, Willie posted respectable batting averages of .273 and .291. In 1962 the team won the pennant, and the seven-game World Series against the Yankees that fall ended with the most memorable at bat in McCovey's 22-year career. It came with two out in the bottom of the ninth inning of the seventh game. The Giants were losing 1–0 but had the tying and winning runs at second and third. McCovey cracked one of Ralph Terry's deliveries on its loudest side and sent a throbbing line drive at second

McCovey in 1979.

Taking his cuts in the batting cage.

baseman Bobby Richardson, who stabbed it. A foot or so in either direction and Willie's drive would have made the Giants world champions; instead, it became the most lethal final out in World Series history.

In 1963 the Giants decided to install McCovey in the regular lineup. Playing a full season (most of it in the outfield), Willie poured it on all year, smashing 44 home runs to tie Henry Aaron for the league lead.

After an off year in 1964, McCovey came back with 39 home runs in 1965, and early the next season the Giants traded Cepeda to the Cardinals, finally opening the first-base job for Willie. Playing the position he was most comfortable in seemed to relax him, and McCovey turned in the most consistently productive seasons of his career. In 1968 and 1969 he led the National League in home runs and runs batted in, joining Chicago's Bill Nicholson as the only man in league history to win back-to-back titles in these elite slugging categories. (Nicholson did it in 1943 and 1944; Mike Schmidt was to do it in 1980 and 1981.) In 1969 Willie, who batted his career high of .320 that year, was voted the National League's Most Valuable Player.

In 1970 Willie hit 39 home runs—the seventh and final time he cleared the 30 mark in long shots—and drove in 126 runs.

McCovey was still turning out solid performances when the Giants traded him to San Diego after the 1973 season. According to stories coming from San Francisco at the time, the Giants were trying to lighten the weight of their payroll; thus within a year's time Willie Mays, Juan Marichal, and McCovey all left the club.

McCovey put in a couple of indifferent years with the Padres, then was sold to the Oakland Athletics near the end of the 1976 season. At the age of thirty-nine, Willie played out his option with the A's, declared free agency, and was re-signed by the Giants in January 1977, a move that some people viewed as sentimental more than anything else. Willie, however, surprised everyone by hitting 28 homers, driving in 86 runs, batting .280, and earning the National League's Comeback Player of the Year award.

After two more years, during which his production fell off considerably, McCovey retired midway through the 1980 season, his 22nd in the big leagues. He was elected to the Hall of Fame in 1986, his first year of eligibility.

Soft-spoken, noncontroversial, McCovey was often overshadowed by the spectacular Mays and the volatile Cepeda. Sometimes, he said, he felt "unappreciated," though he did feel that he was "respected" by other players. That was certainly an understatement, for as Dodger pitcher Don Sutton put it, "He easily was the most feared hitter in the league. He was awesome."

Garvey in 1980.

STEVE GARVEY

It was one of the telltale signs of the times that Steve Garvey's politeness and consideration of others made him a dubious character in the eyes of some of his teammates. Garvey would stop in an airline terminal and put down his luggage and amiably sign autographs; he was unfailingly obliging in giving interviews; he was agreeable when asked to pose for pictures; he spoke in praise of God and country and of virtues that cynics considered passé.

His detractors were skeptical. They said his hair was always too neatly combed and his uniform too clean. They said his impeccable behavior was calculated, that he was laying the foundation for a future career in politics (in some quarters of the country not considered the noblest of callings).

Nevertheless, Garvey seemed genuinely sensitive to the responsibilities (as he perceived them) that came with being a big-league star, responsibilities that he believed embraced the world both within and without the ball park. Referring to his consecutive-game streak that ultimately became a National League record, he said, "It's not just physical, it's spiritual, too. You depend upon a guy to be out there." He wanted to be dependable, he said, "to be counted on to be there every day."

But no one, not the detractors or the cynics, ever denied that this uncompromising individualist could play baseball, that he was one of the finest players of his time. At bat and in the field he was a rugged, durable, reliable performer, and never more so than when under pressure: Many of his performances in World Series and league-championship play were of record-book caliber.

Garvey was born in Tampa, Florida, on December 22, 1948. His father was a driver for the Greyhound Company and during spring training often drove chartered buses for ball clubs, including the Dodgers, for whom young Steve sometimes served as batboy. The experience inculcated in the boy a love for and devotion to the Dodgers. Gil Hodges was his favorite player. "He was a gentleman on and off the field," Garvey recalled. "I always admired him." The coda to Garvey's youthful hero worship was that he grew up to take possession of Hodges' old position with the Dodgers and ultimately to challenge his one-time idol's standing as the greatest of Dodger first basemen.

Garvey could always hit, right from the beginning. He hit in the Little League, in American Legion ball, in high school. He also excelled on the gridiron, showing enough to earn a football scholarship to Michigan State University, where he played in the defensive backfield as well as starting on the baseball team.

Baseball, however, remained his first love, and when in 1968 he was drafted by his favorite team, the Dodgers, he left school to enter pro ball. (He continued his studies in the off-season and in 1971 received a degree in education.)

The Dodgers launched the new man with the Ogden, Utah, club in the Pioneer League, where he batted .338. A year later he was with Albuquerque in the Texas League, batting .373, despite missing several months with a broken hand. The following season he was with the Dodgers' top team, Spokane in the Pacific Coast League, batting .319. The big team knew they had a hitter in the twenty-two-year-old from Tampa, and what particularly caught their attention was his RBI record in three minor-league seasons: 240 games, 231 runs batted in.

But Garvey's nonstop progress to the top was being impeded by his fielding. The man whose glove work was later to set records around first base was being brought along as a third baseman, and throwing from the hot corner was proving to be a problem: His arm was strong but erratic. Nevertheless, the Dodger brass

Garvey rounding first base after hitting his second home run of the game on October 9, 1974, in the league-championship series against Pittsburgh. The jubilant Dodger on the right is Tom Lasorda, then the club's first-base coach.

remained enchanted by the line-drive swing that scorched balls to all fields.

Garvey was with the Dodgers for 34 games in 1970, batting .269. The team tried him at both second and third; his defense was unsatisfactory at either spot. In 1971 and 1972 he was still playing third base, still making too many errors. In 1972 his 28 errors in just 85 games led the league. His batting average was .269, and the club felt he could do much better.

"He obviously wasn't a third baseman," his manager Walter Alston said. "But he obviously was going to be a hitter, and none of us ever gave up on him. I liked him. He was a good, serious kid; he did whatever you asked and always gave a hundred percent. I knew he'd be all right. It was just a matter of time."

In 1973 Alston moved first baseman Bill Buckner to the outfield and handed the big glove to Garvey.

"We couldn't have done it before," Alston said, "because we had Wes Parker, the best fielder in the league, playing first. Then Parker retired after the 1972 season. Then Ron Cey came up, and he was going to be the third baseman. We wanted all these boys in the lineup, so we moved Buckner to the outfield and put Garvey on first base. He took to it right away. He began making all the plays, especially digging out low throws. He was also good at making the sweeping tag play, which sometimes brought him into the path of the runner. He had some pretty rough collisions, but he always bounced right up. I guess that was his old football experience—he was used to getting banged around and wasn't afraid of it. He wasn't afraid of anything. And he started hitting the ball.

In 1973 Garvey batted .304. The year saw the formation of what was to become the most durable infield in baseball history: Garvey at first base, Davey Lopes at second, Bill Russell at short, and Cey at third. The unit remained intact until 1981.

Garvey became a star in 1974, ringing up the impressive statistics that he would maintain through the rest of the decade. He batted .312, collected 200 hits, hit 21 home runs, and drove in 111 runs. He was a write-in starter for the National League in the All-Star Game, where he delivered two key hits and made a spectacular defensive play, for which he was voted the game's MVP. This foreshadowed an even greater distinction that fall—being voted the National League's Most Valuable Player.

Helping the Dodgers to the division title, he then helped them to the pennant

Action at first base in Pittsburgh on July 20, 1978. Garvey is receiving the throw a split second too late to retire the Pirates' Frank Taveras.

The most durable infield unit in major-league history. *Left to right:* Ron Cey, Bill Russell, Davey Lopes, Steve Garvey.

by batting .389 in the club's four-game victory over the Phillies. In the World Series loss to Oakland he batted .381.

Year after year Garvey continued to solidify his stardom. From 1975 through 1980 he logged batting averages of .319, .317, .297, .316, .315, and .304. His hit totals for the same years were uncannily methodical: 210, 200, 192, 202, 204, 200. In four of those years he drove in over 100 runs. In 1977 he reached his home-run peak with 33. In 1975, 1976, and 1977 he led National League first basemen in fielding average (he would lead again in 1981 and 1984). He also began his challenge to pain and injury with an endur-

ance performance that would ultimately establish a new National League record of 1,207 consecutive games.

In 1974, 1977, 1978, and 1981 the Dodgers took division titles and pennants, with Garvey generally excelling in both league-championship matches and World Series. In 1978 he helped demolish the Phillies by hitting four home runs in four games, setting a number of LCS slugging records. His batting average for five league-championship series (including one with the San Diego Padres in 1984) is .356; for five World Series, .319.

Tom Lasorda, who replaced Alston as Dodger manager in 1977 (and who was

Garvey with the San Diego Padres in 1984.

Garvey's first manager in professional ball, with Ogden in 1968), said this of his star first baseman: "He comes to the ball park every day, ready to play. He's ready to give you his best, every day. He doesn't make trouble, he doesn't give anyone a headache, he just does his job." (Precisely the sentiments Joe McCarthy voiced about Lou Gehrig.)

While Lasorda was describing a manager's dream player, some of Garvey's teammates had other opinions, notably pitcher Don Sutton, a freer, more irreverent spirit than Garvey. One day in 1978 the two had a clubhouse confrontation that ended in a brief but violent brawl. For the Dodgers and Lasorda, who was celebrated for preaching the familial togetherness of his team, it was embarrassing. The incident left Garvey unruffled; he went on being himself, a man upholding verities that some people insisted were passé.

After the 1982 season Garvey opted for free agency. When he and the Dodgers could not agree on a contract, he accepted a lucrative offer from the San Diego Padres.

Though his sterling seasons were behind him now, Garvey still performed solidly for his new club, with batting averages of .294, .284, and .281 in 1983, 1984, and 1985. In 1983 a thumb injury brought to an end his consecutive-game streak at 1,207, a new National League record (earlier in the season he had broken Billy Williams' old record of 1,117).

In 1984 Garvey helped the Padres to their first pennant ever, capping his efforts with a ninth-inning, game-winning home run in the league-championship series against the Cubs. The "flawless" player also institutionalized that designation by turning in an impeccable season at first base—161 games without a single error. It was the first time in major-league history that a first baseman had gone through a full season without committing an error. Overall, Garvey had an errorless streak of 193 straight games (a major-league record), from June 26, 1983, to April 14, 1985, during which he handled 1,633 chances (a National League record).

At the end of the 1986 season Garvey held the major-league record for highest fielding average for a first baseman in 1,000 or more games, .996, which, in conjunction with his 2,583 hits and .295 batting average, established him as one of the premier first basemen of all time.

In the age of the nonconformist and the anti-hero, when unappealing traits and foibles drifted through the stardust, Garvey has stood out as a man who blazed his trail very early in life and has continued to follow it faithfully through a long and distinguished career marked throughout by two of the many virtues he prized so highly—consistency and dependability.

Cooper in 1976, the year he was traded to Milwaukee.

CECIL COOPER

"At least we didn't trade him to the Yankees," one Boston Red Sox fan said. And that was just about all the consolation Red Sox supporters could derive when they looked back on the trade that sent Cecil Cooper to the Milwaukee Brewers on December 6, 1976. (Red Sox fans were still haunted by the many unfortunate transactions between their club and the Yankees, beginning with the dispatching to New York of Babe Ruth, Waite Hoyt, Herb Pennock, and Carl Mays in the 1920s, Red Ruffing in 1930, and on up to Sparky Lyle in the early 1970s.)

If Cooper was undervalued by the Red Sox, then it was only symptomatic of what he had to contend with throughout his career. Overshadowed in the league at first base by Eddie Murray (whom he consistently outhit), Cooper had the further misfortune of seeing his greatest year (1980) be completely dominated by George Brett, who rocked the universe of baseball that season with his spectacular .390 batting average.

It was in that 1980 season that Cooper batted .352, hit 25 home runs, banged out 219 hits, and led the league with 122 runs batted in. As outstanding as it all was, it left him little more than an also-ran to Brett.

While Cooper's sparkling season may have caught some fans by surprise, not too many people within the baseball fraternity felt it was out of character. "The guy could always hit," said batting coach Charlie Lau, one of the gurus of modern hitting technique.

A glimpse at Cooper's batting averages from the time he entered professional baseball in 1968 bears out Lau's appraisal. Cecil, in fact, was a hitter from the time he lifted his first bat in Little League and right on through high school. Despite his abilities, Cooper, who was born in Brenham, Texas, on December 20, 1949, did not through childhood indulge the standard dream of playing big-league baseball.

"I never really gave it much thought," he said, "until I was in high school." Then he found himself playing on a few state-

Red Sox rookie Cecil Cooper in 1971.

championship teams, the kind that lures major-league scouts to far-flung diamonds where games are played before modest but enthusiastic crowds in small grandstands.

Cooper was considered a prospect from the start, but even then he was not fully appreciated. It was not until the 27th round of the free-agent draft in June 1968 that the Red Sox selected him. He was signed to a contract and sent to the Jamestown, New York, team in the New York–Penn League. The eighteen-year-old from East Texas was definitely not intimidated by professional pitching: He broke into 26 games and batted a sizzling .452.

Two years later Cooper was with the Danville, Illinois, team in the Midwest League, leading all hitters with a .336 average. That winter the St. Louis Cardinals drafted him, but they were evidently not impressed and returned him to the Red Sox after spring training.

Cooper split the 1971 season between Winston–Salem in the Carolina League, where he batted .379, and Pawtucket, Rhode Island, in the Eastern League, where he batted .343. He finished up the year with the Red Sox, getting into 14 games and batting .310.

He spent most of the 1972 season with Boston's Louisville club in the International League, batting .315. All this earned him, however, was another summer in Pawtucket, where he batted .293. The Red Sox again brought him up late in the season, and in 30 games he batted just .235; nevertheless, he was now in the big leagues to stay.

Over the next three years Cooper divided his time between first base and designated hitter. The stumbling block in front of Cooper was named Carl Yas-

trzemski, who was now playing first base more and more for the Red Sox, and even though Cooper was outhitting the veteran, it was not then possible to move Carl Yastrzemski out of the Red Sox lineup.

After seasons of .275, .311, and .282, Cooper was traded to the Milwaukee Brewers. There was some speculation that the Red Sox had become disenchanted with Cecil after his 1-for-19 performance in the 1975 World Series against Cincinnati, but the basis for the trade was Boston's desire to reacquire first baseman George Scott, whose booming right-handed bat seemed made to order for Fenway Park's short left-field wall. For Boston the trade was a mistake; Scott lasted just two seasons in Fenway,

Cooper in 1987.

A .352 hitter in 1980.

while Cecil Cooper suddenly soared into baseball's stellar regions.

From 1977 through 1983, only two men in baseball batted .300 or over for those seven consecutive seasons—Rod Carew and Cecil Cooper. Wheeling through a comfortable gilt-edged rut, Cooper batted .300, .312, .308, .352, .320, .313, and .307. Four times during this period the Milwaukee first baseman cleared the 100 RBI mark: 106 in 1979, a league-leading 122 in 1980, 121 in 1982, and 126 in 1983, again a league-leading total.

Cooper was particularly dangerous because he drove the ball to all fields with authority. In 1982 and 1983 he hit 32 and 30 home runs, respectively, at the same time averaging well over 30 doubles a year; he topped the league with 44 two-baggers in 1979 and again with 35 in 1981, the latter quite an impressive total in light of the players' strike that limited the season to just two-thirds of its schedule. Cooper also went over the 200-hit mark three times, with 219 in his big 1980 season being his career high.

Not the snappiest of fielders when he came to the big leagues, Cooper worked diligently to improve this aspect of his game, to the point where the *Sporting News* named him on its American League All-Star fielding team in 1979 and 1980.

In 1982 Cooper was one of the key men in the lineup known as "Harvey's Wall Bangers"—skipper Harvey Kuenn's slugging Milwaukee Brewers that edged the Baltimore Orioles by one game for the American League East title. Cooper turned in one of his strongest and most consistent seasons, only to find himself once again overshadowed, this time by teammate Robin Yount, who turned in an eye-catching MVP season.

It was Cooper, however, who delivered the key hit in Milwaukee's league-championship series showdown with the Western Division winners, the California Angels. The blow came in the bottom of the seventh inning of the fifth and deciding game.

The Brewers had fought back from a 2–0 deficit in games to tie the series. Going into the bottom of the seventh of the final game, they were losing 3–2. They loaded the bases with two out, bringing up Cooper, who had thus far been laboring under a disappointing 2-for-19 series. With the count 1–1, Cecil slammed what he later described as "the most satisfying hit of my life," a two-run single to left field, driving in the runs that gave the Brewers a 4–3 victory and their first American League pennant. The clutch single has been described as the most momentous hit in Milwaukee Brewers history, and, appropriately, it was delivered by one of the fine hitters of his era.

Hernandez in 1986, the year he helped drive the Mets to the world championship.

KEITH HERNANDEZ

During the New York Mets' power-house drive to the National League pennant and world championship in 1986, one observer wrote, "Keith Hernandez is keeping the instant-replay technicians working overtime this season." The reference was, of course, to the Mets' first baseman's breathtaking performances around first base, during which he was making the phenomenal look routine. Whether it was going to his right or his left, making the 3–6–3 double play, charging bunts, or digging out low throws, Hernandez continued to set and maintain the highest standards for playing first base. These highly polished, highly consistent executions had been going on for years; Hernandez was the winner of nine straight Gold Glove awards, from 1978 through 1986.

A San Francisco product, Hernandez was born on October 20, 1953, son of a minor-league infielder who became the boy's first baseball instructor and later his most astute critic. (John Hernandez once was watching his slump-ridden son on television, immediately picked up the slight flaw in Keith's stance, and, like ridding the system of a bacteria, made him well again.)

Hernandez attended Capuchino High School, where he proved himself a gifted, multitalented athlete, the first ever in the school's history to make all-league in baseball, basketball, and football, where he quarterbacked the team.

The seventeen-year-old Hernandez was a 42nd-round choice of the St. Louis Cardinals in the June 1971 free-agent draft. He began his professional career in 1972 with St. Petersburg in the Florida State League, breaking in with a .256 batting average.

A year later he batted .260 with the Arkansas club of the Texas League, moving up toward the end of the season to the American Association, where he batted .333 in 31 games with Tulsa.

"We were watching him come along," one Cardinal scout said later, "and could hardly wait. We badly needed a regular first baseman, but we didn't want to rush Keith too fast."

In 1974, the twenty-year-old Hernandez

113

At bat: Keith Hernandez.

was with Tulsa all year and led the American Association with a .351 batting average. Brought up to St. Louis at the end of the season, he played in 14 games and batted .294.

The Cardinals decided to give him one more year at Tulsa. After 85 games, with Hernandez batting .330, the big team reasoned the boy had had all the seasoning he needed and brought him up to St. Louis for keeps. In 64 games the rookie batted .250.

Over the next three years, Hernandez batted .289, .291, and .255.

"That .255 didn't faze anybody," said a member of the St. Louis front office. "You just had a comfortable feeling about the guy. He was one hell of an intelligent player. It was just a matter of him getting it all together. You knew it was going to happen."

It happened a year later, in 1979, when the twenty-five-year-old Hernandez had his greatest season to date. He won the batting championship with a .344 average, led with 48 doubles and 116 runs scored, drove in 105 runs, and collected 210 hits, in addition to taking the second of his nine straight Gold Gloves. That fall there was an unprecedented tie for the Most Valuable Player award, Hernandez sharing it with Pittsburgh's Willie Stargell.

Hernandez followed this superb season in 1980 with a .321 batting average (three points behind the leader, Bill Buckner), rapping out 191 hits, driving in 99 runs, and again leading the league in runs scored, with 111.

Hernandez continued his consistent play over the next two years, batting .306 in 1981 and .299 in 1982, the year the Cardinals won the National League pennant and the world championship. Keith

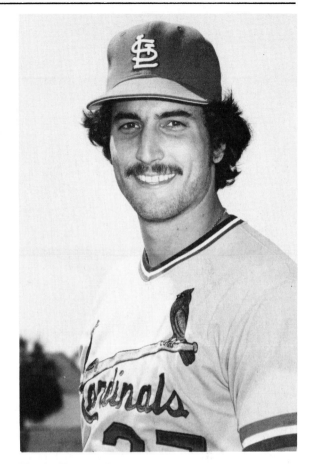

Keith Hernandez in 1977.

started out in still waters in the seven-game World Series against the Milwaukee Brewers, going hitless in the first four games; but then he snapped into gear and finished with a rush, getting seven hits and driving in eight runs over the last three games as the Cardinals emerged as champions.

That was in October 1982. Less than a year later, on June 15, 1983, the world came crumbling down around Hernandez. Called into manager Whitey Herzog's office that night, on the eve of the trading deadline, Hernandez, to his astonishment and dismay, was told, "We traded you."

Hernandez *(right)* and Steve Garvey.

Mets first baseman Keith Hernandez making the play.

When he heard he had been dealt to the Mets, Hernandez went into the shower and cried. Not only had he been traded away from a world-championship team, but the deal was sending him, in his own words, to "the Siberia of baseball." At that point in their history the Mets had reverted to their original incarnation of chronic losers—six last- or next-to-last-place moorings in the previous six years. An inept, lethargic, laughably bad team.

Hernandez's first impulse was not to report, but eventually he packed his bags and headed east. He resolved to do the best he could, pile up good statistics, and escape by declaring free agency after the 1984 season.

The Mets management, however, convinced him the club was serious about building a winner, had some exceptionally talented youngsters on the way, and were on the brink of success. The first two selling points were absolutely true; the third depended to a large extent on Hernandez. He remained, signing a lucrative long-term contract.

Splitting the 1983 season between St. Louis and New York, Hernandez batted .297. A year later, with the Mets finishing second, he batted .311. In 1985, the team was in contention until the next-to-last game of the season, as Keith batted .309 and drove in 91 runs, the sixth time in his career he had bettered the 90 mark in RBIs.

In 1986 it all fell into place for the New York Mets. Sparked by Hernandez, the club's hard-driving field leader, the Mets battered their way through the league, the league championship series against Houston, and finally their memorable, almost theatrical World Series victory over Boston.

Hernandez had become a paragon of consistency; after years in which he batted .311 and .309, he hit .310 in the world-championship year (the sixth time in eight years he had cleared the .300 mark). In leading National League first basemen in fielding percentage for the second straight year, he also won that ninth consecutive Gold Glove.

By now New York fans had become accustomed to Hernandez's intense, often spectacular defensive play around first base. He had expanded the range of the position so that it extended from the outfield grass clear to the third-base line, where he sped in to pick up bunts and execute force plays at third base. As New York fans had come out generations before to watch Hal Chase spin pirouettes around first base at old Hilltop Park, so were they coming now to watch the greatest defensive first baseman of his era perform his magic at Shea Stadium.

The all-around potency of Hernandez was summed up in a question one fan asked another as they were leaving Shea one night: "Do you think Hernandez knocks in more runs with his bat or saves more runs with his glove?"

Both feet off the ground, Murray handling a tricky hop.

EDDIE MURRAY

In an age when star athletes are interviewed, analyzed, photographed, tape recorded, and generally publicized with unrelenting fervor, Eddie Murray, superstar first baseman of the Baltimore Orioles, has sought anonymity. It wasn't star temperament or a churlish disposition.

"He's shy," said a teammate. "He's just plain shy."

Shyness is almost always ambiguously perceived; it can offend a stranger and frustrate a journalist; it is often interpreted as arrogance, hostility, hauteur, aloofness, anything but what it is. Teammates say that in the clubhouse and around the batting cage, Murray is as rollicking as anyone on the club; but if a stranger should appear, he immediately chills over.

On the field Murray is an utterly relaxed performer, to the extent that in his early years his teammates called him "Tired." This, of course, was one of baseball's antithetical nicknames, for no one on the club was quicker at the plate or more alertly in the game.

"If you didn't know who he was," one American League pitcher said, "he could deceive the hell out of you; he's so laid-back and easy-going. But once he sets himself at the plate and narrows those big eyes and looks out at you, you know you've got your hands full." Indeed, in a poll taken among American League pitchers in the early 1980s, Murray was selected by more pitchers as the batter they least liked to see at the plate in a tense situation. The consensus was that Murray responded to pressure as well as any man in the league.

Murray was born on February 24, 1956, in Los Angeles, one of five boys and seven girls, member of a spirited, extremely close-knit family that was drawn even closer by that good old American elixir, baseball. The brothers and sisters played ball in empty lots and playgrounds and, on rainy days, in the family garage, swatting away at baseballs and anything else that might be employed to impersonate a ball—rolled-up socks, tin cans, even some of the girls' old dolls.

All this hyperactivity sent two of the

119

brothers to the major leagues (Eddie's brother Rich played briefly with the San Francisco Giants) and three into the minor leagues.

After his graduation from Locke High School in 1973 (where Ozzie Smith was a teammate), Eddie received a $20,000 bonus to sign with the Orioles. The O's broke him in with Bluefield, West Virginia, in the Appalachian League, where in 50 games he batted .287 and hit 11 home runs.

A year later he batted .289 for Miami in the Florida State League, earning another promotion in 1975 to Asheville, North Carolina, in the Southern League, where he batted .264 and hit 17 home runs. Up to this point, the man who was to become the greatest power-hitting switch-hitter since Mickey Mantle was strictly a right-handed batter. Late in the season, after becoming increasingly frustrated by right-handed curve balls, Murray started switching at the plate. The experiment was such an immediate suc-

Demonstrating a new way of holding a runner on. The unsuspecting base runner is Minnesota's Roy Smalley.

cess that it was hardly an experiment at all, lending weight to Eddie's quietly stated credo, "You have to adjust."

Murray split the 1976 season between Charlotte, North Carolina, in the Southern League and Rochester in the International League, batting .298 and .274, respectively. By this time the organization considered him a can't-miss prospect. However, in the opinion of the Baltimore hierarchy, the twenty-year-old slugger needed one more year of seasoning at Rochester. That opinion underwent radical alteration in spring training 1977, when manager Earl Weaver heard "the sound."

The sound was the crisp, loud impact of Murray putting the bat on the ball in the batting cage. A big-league manager's ears are as keenly attuned to that sound as a maestro's are to the nuances of his orchestra, and what Weaver was hearing "made me turn around and look." It was the resonance of contact and power. It

Eddie Murray.

Murray in the cage during batting practice.

sounded enough times that spring for Murray to make the team, and it continued to reverberate through the American League all summer with enough regularity to earn the Baltimore youngster Rookie of the Year honors.

In his first season, Murray batted .283, hit 27 home runs, and drove in 88 RBIs. It was the beginning of his year in, year out amassing of high-powered statistics, the uniformity of which finally began to make him look programmed. His home runs, runs batted in, and batting averages for the first 10 years of his career read like this:

Year	HR	RBI	BAV
1977	27	88	.283
1978	27	95	.285
1979	25	99	.295
1980	32	116	.300
1981	22	78	.294 (strike year)
1982	32	110	.316
1983	33	111	.306
1984	29	110	.306
1985	31	124	.297
1986	17	84	.305

As an indication of the increasing respect pitchers were developing for him, Murray twice led the league in intentional walks, in 1982 with 18 and in 1984 with 25. And three times the quiet man has explosively signaled his potency at the plate, hitting three home runs in a game on August 29, 1979, September 14, 1980, and August 26, 1985.

A complete ballplayer, Murray is considered one of the most adept defensive first basemen in baseball; in the truncated 1981 season he made just one error in 99 games for a .999 fielding average. According to day in, day out observers, he has no peer when it comes to execut-

Dodger manager Tom Lasorda *(center)* posing with the American League's two best first basemen at the 1982 All-Star Game, Cecil Cooper *(left)* and Eddie Murray.

ing the difficult 3–6–3 double play. Brooks Robinson has called him the best he has ever seen at fielding bunts and forcing a runner at second.

There are some who maintain that Murray's self-effacing personality has caused him to be underrated. But these "underraters," whoever they are, are surely not to be found among the fans at Baltimore's Memorial Stadium, who begin fervent chants of *Eddie, Eddie* when their great first baseman comes to the plate with runners in scoring position.

Don Mattingly in the batting cage: all business.

DON MATTINGLY

Considering that Don Mattingly has played just a few years of major-league ball, including him among the game's greatest first basemen might seem immoderate. Nevertheless, certain judgments must be made in part on faith, and when in 1986 it was the common opinion among those who played and followed big-league ball that Mattingly was the game's premier player, it gave that act of faith a substantial bolstering. To many, that professional assessment of Mattingly's talents was a more impressive accolade than the Most Valuable Player award he was voted after the 1985 season.

One of the many things the Yankee first baseman quickly became known for was his exemplary work habits. The diligence with which he applied himself to perfecting his stance and his swing did not go unnoticed.

"He can get three hits in a game and still be dissatisfied," one Yankee coach said, "and come out early the next day and spend an hour or so in the batting cage. Most hitters, if they get three hits in a game, feel good later on. Mattingly wants to feel good—that is, comfortable and right—*while* he's doing it."

One American League coach said of Mattingly: "He's one of the few guys who seems genuinely surprised when he doesn't get a hit. That's the kind of concentration and self-confidence he brings with him to the plate. It's not an ego thing, it's that he's concentrating so hard on getting that hit. You see the same thing in guys like Wade Boggs and George Brett. In the great ones."

This self-confidence, this resolve and intensity, was never more evident than in the final game of the 1984 season. When the game started, Mattingly and teammate Dave Winfield were in a race for the league batting title, with Winfield ahead by two points, .341 to .339. Winfield went 1-for-4, while Mattingly, in a truly blazing performance, rapped out four hits in five at bats to take the title, .343 to .340. It was the most scorching finish-line display seen in many years.

Don Mattingly, who in his early twenties was already being compared to such previous Yankee icons as Babe Ruth, Lou Gehrig, Joe DiMaggio, and Mickey Mantle, was born in Evansville, Indiana, on April 21, 1961. He was a standout on the Evansville Memorial High School baseball team (a team he helped to a 49-game winning streak) as a pitcher and a hitter. Some scouts thought he had potential as a pitcher, but as Mattingly later put it, "I didn't want to pitch. I was a hitter." Succinct and correct.

Because the Detroit Tigers had a farm club in Evansville, the Tigers were Mattingly's first love. As he sat in the minor-league grandstand watching young players like Jack Morris, Lance Parrish, and Dan Petry rise from Evansville to the Tigers, the youngster dreamed of one day joining them in Detroit.

The early scouting reports on Mattingly rated him too slow to be considered a prospect for professional ball. (Lack of exceptional running speed remains the only soft spot in the Mattingly armor.) Another factor that discouraged teams from selecting him in the June 1979 amateur draft was the boy's stated desire to go to college.

But the Yankees were interested, not fervently interested, but enough to draft him in the 19th round (meaning that some 450 players had been chosen ahead of him) and enough to offer the seventeen-year-old a $22,000 bonus. He accepted, deciding to postpone college.

Mattingly began his ascent to stardom with the Oneonta, New York, team in the New York–Pennsylvania League, breaking in with what was to become the Mattingly hallmark—a smoking bat. In 53 games, the rookie, primarily an outfielder then, batted .349. A year later,

"The best all-around player in baseball."

playing for Greensboro, North Carolina, he led the South Atlantic League with a .358 batting average, and the Yankees began to take notice.

After a .316 season with Nashville in the Southern Association in 1981, Mattingly was promoted in 1982 to the Yankees' top farm club, Columbus, in the International League, where he maintained the tattoo, batting .315.

Mattingly opened the 1983 season with the Yankees, but because of the plethora of high-priced players on the club, skipper Billy Martin was forced to send the youngster back to Columbus. Breaking news of this nature to a young player is, most managers concede, the toughest part of their job. Players have been known to sulk or rage or cry when informed. According to Martin, when Mat-

Mattingly in spring training, 1984.

tingly was told of the demotion, he simply replied, "I'll be back soon."

And he was, after 43 games and a .340 batting average. Finishing out the season with the Yankees (dividing his time between the outfield and first base), the rookie batted .283, a late-season slump costing him the .300 average he had always maintained.

The leap to superstardom occurred the following season, in 1984. Mattingly won his batting title with a superb all-around offensive output. Accompanying his .343 average were 23 home runs, 110 runs batted in, and league-leading figures in hits (207) and doubles (44). In 603 at bats he struck out just 33 times.

In 1985 he improved in every category except batting average. While his average dropped to .324, Mattingly put on a power burst with 35 home runs and league-leading totals in runs batted in (145), doubles (48), and total bases (370), all of it stitched together with 211 hits. Mattingly's RBI total was the highest in the American League since Al Rosen had driven in the same number for Cleveland in 1953. This was the kind of high batting average and robust slugging achieved by those previous Yankee demigods Ruth, Gehrig, DiMaggio, and Mantle. And showing his completeness as a player was Mattingly's .995 fielding percentage, highest among American League first basemen.

Mattingly at bat in Yankee Stadium, 1986.

Having already achieved what for most players would have been pinnacle career numbers, Mattingly went ahead in 1986 and improved on some of them. He batted .352 (though he was nosed out for the title by Boston's Wade Boggs), led in hits with 238, for the third straight time in doubles with 53, for the second straight time in total bases with 388, and took his first slugging title with a .573 mark. He was now clearly the Yankees' greatest first baseman since the heyday of Gehrig, nearly a half century before.

Mattingly seemed resolved not to permit himself an off year, the letdown season that sometimes afflicts the achiever of glittering statistics. If the soft-spoken Yankee hitting machine had a credo, he uttered it after winning his batting crown in 1984:

"I can still improve. The key is to never be satisfied. Push farther than you think might be your limit."

Yankee rookie Don Mattingly in 1983.

"The best all-around player in baseball."

"THEY ALSO RAN"

For a list of the "best" or "greatest" to be truly meaningful, it must be finite, limited by certain standards. Consequently, as in the list of first basemen under discussion in this book, there are many outstanding names whose exclusion may strike some as errors of judgment. Most prominent among those players are the following:

Hal Trosky, Cleveland slugger of the 1930s. Over a career that was shortened by illness, Trosky batted .302. Four times he batted .330 or better, including his best all-around year, 1936, when he batted .343, hit 42 home runs, led the American League with 162 runs batted in, and collected 216 hits. He had six straight years of over 100 RBIs (1934–39) and was only twenty-nine years old when severe migraine headaches all but brought his career to an end.

Joe Adcock, who played for Cincinnati, Milwaukee, Cleveland, and the Los Angeles–California Angels from 1950 through 1966. He had a lifetime total of 336 home runs, with a high of 38 in 1956.

Norm Cash, who came up with the White Sox in 1958 but spent the bulk of his career, until his retirement in 1974, with Detroit. Cash hit over .300 just once, but it was a league-leading .361 in 1961, a year in which he hit 41 home runs and drove in 132 runs. The following year he hit 39 home runs, his second-best total. Overall, Cash had 377 career home runs.

Frank McCormick, Cincinnati's premier first baseman just before World War II. McCormick, who led the National League in hits for his first three seasons in the majors (1938–40) while batting .327, .332, and .309 and was MVP in 1940, had his career seriously impeded by a back injury. He played with the Reds, Phillies, and Braves until 1948, batting over .300 six seasons, with a .299 lifetime average.

Jake Daubert, who played for Brooklyn and Cincinnati from 1910 through 1924 (he died at the age of forty a few weeks after the end of the 1924 season). "Gentleman Jake," as he was known, was a lifetime .303 hitter who won batting titles with Brooklyn in 1913 and 1914 with averages of .350 and .329. Jake batted over .300 ten seasons.

Tony Perez, who spent 23 years in the major leagues, with Cincinnati, Montreal, Boston, and Philadelphia, from 1964 through 1986. Perez was one of the most dependable RBI men of his time, driving in 90 or more twelve seasons, including 11 years in a row, from 1967 through 1977.

Boog Powell, Baltimore's hard-hitting MVP in 1970. Powell was with the Orioles from 1961 through 1974, with Cleveland for two years, and finished up with the Dodgers in 1975. Powell hit a career total of 339 home runs, with highs of 39 in 1964 and 37 in 1969.

Rudy York, who played with the Tigers, Red Sox, White Sox, and Athletics from 1934 to 1948. Primarily a Tiger star, Rudy hit 35 homers in his rookie year of 1935, and in 1943 led the league with 34 home runs and 118 RBIs. He drove in over 100 runs a season six times, with 134 in 1940 being his high. He hit 277 home runs lifetime.

Since baseball debate is inexhaustible and vehemently opinionated, there is no doubt that any knowledgeable fan can emend the roster of primary selections and extend the list of secondary choices.

LIFETIME RECORDS

(Statistics reprinted by permission of the *Sporting News*)

Frank Chance

Year	Club	League	Pos.	G.	AB.	R.	H.	2B.	3B.	HR.	SB.	B.A.	PO.	A.	E.	F.A.
1898—Chicago	Nat.	C-OF	42	146	32	42	2	3	1	5	.288	85	20	8	.929
1899—Chicago	Nat.	C	57	190	36	55	6	2	1	11	.289	165	66	12	.951
1900—Chicago	Nat.	C	48	151	26	46	8	4	0	9	.305	160	64	17	.929
1901—Chicago	Nat.	C	63	228	37	66	11	4	0	30	.289	63	7	5	.933
1902—Chicago	Nat.	C-1B-O	67	236	40	67	8	4	1	28	.284	503	45	15	.978
1903—Chicago	Nat.	1B	123	441	83	144	24	10	2	67	.327	1204	68	36	.972
1904—Chicago	Nat.	1B	124	451	89	140	16	10	6	42	.310	1205	106	13	.990
1905—Chicago	Nat.	1B	115	392	92	124	16	12	2	38	.316	1165	75	13	.990
1906—Chicago	Nat.	1B	136	474	103	151	24	10	3	57	.319	1376	82	16	.989
1907—Chicago	Nat.	1B	109	382	58	112	19	2	1	35	.293	1129	80	10	.992
1908—Chicago	Nat.	1B	126	452	65	123	27	4	2	27	.272	1291	86	15	.989
1909—Chicago	Nat.	1B	92	324	53	88	16	4	0	29	.272	901	40	6	.994
1910—Chicago	Nat.	1B	87	295	54	88	12	8	0	16	.298	773	38	3	.996
1911—Chicago	Nat.	1B	29	88	23	21	6	3	1	9	.239	289	11	3	.990
1912—Chicago	Nat.	1B	2	5	2	1	0	0	0	1	.200	22	0	0	1.000
1913—New York	Amer.	1B	11	24	3	5	0	0	0	1	.208	88	4	0	1.000
1914—New York	Amer.	1B	1	0	0	0	0	0	0	0	.000	1	0	0	1.000
American League Totals			12	24	3	5	0	0	0	1	.208	89	4	0	1.000
National League Totals			1220	4255	793	1268	195	80	20	404	.298	10331	788	172	.985
Major League Totals			1232	4279	796	1273	195	80	20	405	.297	10420	792	172	.985

Hal Chase

Year	Club	League	Pos.	G.	AB.	R.	H.	2B.	3B.	HR.	RBI.	B.A.	PO.	A.	E.	F.A.
1903—Victoria	S.W.W.	1B	52	.....	...	...	...	...	...	.....	.923	....	.....	...	....
1904—Los Angeles	P.C.	1B	173	702	78	196	32	6	2	.....	.279	1482	101	49	.970
1905—New York	Amer.	1B	126	465	60	116	15	6	0	.....	.249	1174	61	31	.976
1906—New York	Amer.	1B	151	597	84	193	25	12	0	.....	.323	1507	89	33	.980
1907—New York	Amer.	1B	125	498	72	143	23	3	2	64	.287	1144	77	34	.973
1908—New York	Amer.	1B	106	405	50	104	11	3	1	31	.257	1020	54	22	.980
1908—Stockton	Cal.St.	1B	21	81	20	31	...	...	...	.....	.383	....	.....	...	....
1909—New York	Amer.	1B	118	474	60	134	17	3	4	62	.283	1202	71	28	.978
1910—New York	Amer.	1B	130	524	67	152	20	5	3	73	.290	1373	65	28	.981
1911—New York	Amer.	1B	133	527	82	166	32	7	3	56	.315	1257	82	36	.974
1912—New York	Amer.	1B	131	522	61	143	21	9	4	52	.274	1162	70	27	.979
1913—N. Y.-Chicago	Amer.	1B	141	530	65	141	13	14	2	52	.266	1334	87	33	.977
1914—Chicago	Amer.	1B	58	206	27	55	10	5	0	23	.267	632	43	13	.981
1914—Buffalo	Fed.	1B	75	291	43	103	19	9	3	.....	.354	691	38	14	.981
1915—Buffalo	Fed.	1B	145	566	85	161	33	10	17	.....	.284	1452	84	23	.985
1916—Cincinnati	Nat.	1-2-OF	142	542	66	184	29	12	4	84	.339	1023	86	20	.982
1917—Cincinnati	Nat.	1B	152	602	71	167	28	15	4	96	.277	1499	80	28	.983
1918—Cincinnati	Nat.	1B	74	259	30	78	12	6	2	37	.301	607	38	13	.980
1919—New York	Nat.	1B	110	408	58	116	17	7	5	54	.284	1205	65	21	.984
Major League Totals			1697	6559	853	1892	273	103	34	.....	.288	16139	968	367	.979

Stuffy McInnis

Year Club League	Pos.	G.	AB.	R.	H.	2B.	3B.	HR.	RBI.	B.A.	PO.	A.	E.	F.A.
1908—Haverhill..................N.Eng.	2B	51	186	24	56	8	3	0	.....	.301	113	147	18	.935
1909—Philadelphia ....Amer.	SS	19	46	4	11	0	0	1	4	.239	34	46	9	.899
1910—Philadelphia ....Amer.	SS	38	73	10	22	2	4	0	12	.301	20	31	4	.927
1911—Philadelphia ....Am.	SS-1B	126	468	76	150	20	10	3	79	.321	1105	101	35	.972
1912—Philadelphia ....Amer.	1B	153	568	83	186	25	13	3	103	.327	1533	100	27	.984
1913—Philadelphia ....Amer.	1B	148	543	79	177	30	4	4	93	.326	1504	79	12	.992
1914—Philadelphia ....Amer.	1B	149	576	74	181	12	8	1	91	.314	1423	85	7	.995
1915—Philadelphia ....Amer.	1B	119	456	44	143	14	4	0	48	.314	1123	83	13	.989
1916—Philadelphia ....Amer.	1B	140	512	42	151	25	3	1	56	.295	1404	96	12	.992
1917—Philadelphia ....Amer.	1B	150	567	50	172	19	4	0	46	.303	1658	95	12	.993
1918—Boston......................Amer.	1-3B	117	423	40	115	11	5	0	58	.272	1100	113	10	.992
1919—Boston......................Amer.	1B	120	440	32	134	12	5	1	60	.305	1236	82	7	.995
1920—Boston......................Amer.	1B	148	559	50	166	21	3	2	71	.297	1586	91	7	.996
1921—Boston......................Amer.	1B	152	584	72	179	31	10	0	74	.307	1549	102	1	.999
1922—Cleveland ....Amer.	1B	142	537	58	164	28	7	1	78	.305	1376	73	5	.997
1923—Boston......................Nat.	1B	154	607	70	191	23	9	2	95	.315	1500	89	14	.991
1924—Boston......................Nat.	1B	146	581	57	169	23	7	1	59	.291	1435	95	10	.994
1925—Pittsburgh ....Nat.	1B	59	155	19	57	10	4	0	24	.368	377	24	3	.993
1926—Pittsburgh ....Nat.	1B	47	127	12	38	6	1	0	13	.299	300	17	4	.988
1927—Philadelphia ....Nat.	1B	1	0	0	0	0	0	0	0	.000	0	0	0	.000
1928—Salem ....N.Eng.	1B	38	115	10	39	5	2	0	17	.339	286	23	3	.990
American League Totals..............................		1721	6352	714	1951	250	80	17	873	.307	16651	1177	161	.991
National League Totals		407	1470	158	455	62	21	3	191	.309	3612	225	31	.992
Major League Totals....................................		2128	7822	872	2406	312	101	20	1064	.308	20263	1402	192	.991

George Sisler

Year Club League	Pos.	G.	AB.	R.	H.	2B.	3B.	HR.	RBI.	B.A.	PO.	A.	E.	F.A.
1915—St. Louis ....Amer.	P-1-O	81	274	28	78	10	2	3	29	.285	413	38	7	.985
1916—St. Louis ....Amer.	1-P-O	151	580	83	177	21	11	4	74	.305	1493	86	24	.985
1917—St. Louis ....Amer.	O-1B	135	539	60	190	30	9	2	55	.353	1384	101	22	.985
1918—St. Louis ....Amer.	1B	114	452	69	154	21	9	2	45	.341	1244	97	13	.990
1919—St. Louis ....Amer.	1B	132	511	96	180	31	15	10	83	.352	1249	120	13	.991
1920—St. Louis ....Amer.	1B	154	631	137	257	49	18	19	122	.407	1477	140	16	.990
1921—St. Louis ....Amer.	1B	138	582	125	216	38	18	12	104	.371	1267	108	10	.993
1922—St. Louis ....Amer.	1B	142	586	134	246	42	18	8	105	.420	1293	125	17	.988
1923—St. Louis ....Amer.						(Out with eye trouble)								
1924—St. Louis ....Amer.	1B	151	636	94	194	27	10	9	74	.305	1326	112	23	.984
1925—St. Louis ....Amer.	1B	150	649	100	224	21	15	12	105	.345	1343	131	26	.983
1926—St. Louis ....Amer.	1B	150	613	78	178	21	12	7	71	.289	1467	87	21	.987
1927—St. Louis ....Amer.	1B	149	614	87	201	32	8	5	97	.327	1374	131	24	.984
1928—Washington..............Amer.	1B	20	49	1	12	1	0	0	2	.245	45	0	0	1.000
1928—Boston......................Nat.	1B	118	491	71	167	26	4	4	68	.340	1188	86	15	.988
1929—Boston......................Nat.	1B	154	629	67	205	40	8	2	79	.326	1398	111	28	.982
1930—Boston......................Nat.	1B	116	431	54	133	15	7	3	67	.309	915	81	13	.987
1931—Rochester ....Int.	1B	159	613	86	186	37	5	3	81	.303	1401	125	20	.987
1932—Shrev.-Tyler ....Texas	1B	70	258	28	74	15	2	1	23	.287	637	33	15	.978
American League Totals..............................		1667	6716	1092	2307	344	145	93	966	.344	15375	1276	216	.987
National League Totals		388	1551	192	505	81	19	9	214	.326	3501	278	56	.985
Major League Totals....................................		2055	8267	1284	2812	425	164	102	1180	.340	18876	1554	272	.987

Jim Bottomley

Year	Club	League	Pos.	G.	AB.	R.	H.	2B.	3B.	HR.	RBI.	B.A.	PO.	A.	E.	F.A.
1920—Sioux City	West.		1B	6	14	0	1	0	0	0	0	.071	35	1	0	1.000
1920—Mitchell	S. Dak.		1B	97	378	69	118	...	...	7	.....	.312	1110	37	15	.987
1921—Houston	Tex.		1B-2B	130	459	50	104	16	5	4	62	.227	1114	59	27	.978
1922—Syracuse	Int.		1B	119	460	78	160	29	15	14	94	.348	1245	61	10	.992
1922—St. Louis	Nat.		1B	37	151	29	49	8	5	5	35	.325	346	12	5	.986
1923—St. Louis	Nat.		1B	134	523	79	194	34	14	8	94	.371	1264	43	18	.986
1924—St. Louis	Nat.		1B	137	528	87	167	31	12	14	111	.316	1297	48	24	.982
1925—St. Louis	Nat.		1B	153	619	92	227	44	12	21	128	.367	1466	74	21	.987
1926—St. Louis	Nat.		1B	154	603	98	180	40	14	19	120	.299	1607	54	19	.989
1927—St. Louis	Nat.		1B	152	574	95	174	31	15	19	124	.303	1656	70	20	.989
1928—St. Louis	Nat.		1B	149	576	123	187	42	20	31	136	.325	1454	52	20	.987
1929—St. Louis	Nat.		1B	146	560	108	176	31	12	29	137	.314	1347	75	13	.991
1930—St. Louis	Nat.		1B	131	487	92	148	33	7	15	97	.304	1164	41	12	.990
1931—St. Louis	Nat.		1B	108	382	73	133	34	5	9	75	.348	897	43	12	.987
1932—St. Louis	Nat.		1B	91	311	45	92	16	3	11	48	.296	662	41	10	.986
1933—Cincinnati	Nat.		1B	145	549	57	137	23	9	13	83	.250	1511	72	15	.991
1934—Cincinnati	Nat.		1B	142	556	72	158	31	11	11	78	.284	1303	77	15	.989
1935—Cincinnati	Nat.		1B	107	399	44	103	21	1	1	49	.258	934	53	8	.992
1936—St. Louis	Amer.		1B	140	544	72	162	39	11	12	95	.298	1250	47	10	.992
1937—St. Louis	Amer.		1B	65	109	11	26	7	0	1	12	.239	179	12	1	.995
1938—Syracuse	Int.		1B	7	14	0	1	0	0	0	0	.071	31	0	1	.969
American League Totals				205	653	83	188	46	11	13	107	.288	1429	59	11	.993
National League Totals				1786	6818	1094	2125	419	140	206	1315	.312	16908	755	212	.988
Major League Totals				1991	7471	1177	2313	465	151	219	1422	.310	18337	814	223	.988

Lou Gehrig

Year	Club	League	Pos.	G.	AB.	R.	H.	2B.	3B.	HR.	RBI.	B.A.	PO.	A.	E.	F.A.
1921—Hartford*	East.		1B	12	46	5	12	1	2	0	.....	.261	130	4	2	.985
1922—								(Not in Organized Ball)								
1923—New York	Amer.		1B-PH	13	26	6	11	4	1	1	9	.423	53	3	4	.933
1923—Hartford	East.		1B	59	227	54	69	13	8	24	.....	.304	623	23	6	.991
1924—New York	Amer.		PH-1-O	10	12	2	6	1	0	0	5	.500	10	1	0	1.000
1924—Hartford	East.		1B	134	504	111	186	40	13	37	.....	.369	1391	66	23	.984
1925—New York	Amer.		1B-OF	126	437	73	129	23	10	20	68	.295	1126	53	13	.989
1926—New York	Amer.		1B	155	572	135	179	47	20	16	107	.313	1565	73	15	.991
1927—New York	Amer.		1B	155	584	149	218	52	18	47	175	.373	1662	88	15	.992
1928—New York	Amer.		1B	154	562	139	210	47	13	27	142	.374	1488	79	18	.989
1929—New York	Amer.		1B	154	553	127	166	33	9	35	126	.300	1458	82	9	.994
1930—New York	Amer.		1B-OF	154	581	143	220	42	17	41	174	.379	1298	89	15	.989
1931—New York	Amer.		1B-OF	155	619	163	211	31	15	46	184	.341	1352	58	13	.991
1932—New York	Amer.		1B	156	596	138	208	42	9	34	151	.349	1293	75	18	.987
1933—New York	Amer.		1B	152	593	138	198	41	12	32	139	.334	1290	64	9	.993
1934—New York	Amer.		1B-SS	154	579	128	210	40	6	49	165	.363	1284	80	8	.994
1935—New York	Amer.		1B	149	535	125	176	26	10	30	119	.329	1337	82	15	.990
1936—New York	Amer.		1B	155	579	167	205	37	7	49	152	.354	1377	82	9	.994
1937—New York	Amer.		1B	157	569	138	200	37	9	37	159	.351	1370	74	16	.989
1938—New York	Amer.		1B	157	576	115	170	32	6	29	114	.295	1483	100	14	.991
1939—New York	Amer.		1B	8	28	2	4	0	0	0	1	.143	64	4	2	.971
Major League Totals				2164	8001	1888	2721	535	162	493	1990	.340	19511	1087	193	.991

Bill Terry

Year Club	League	Pos.	G.	AB.	R.	H.	2B.	3B.	HR.	RBI.	B.A.	PO.	A.	E.	F.A.
1915—Newnan	Ga.-Ala.	P	8	.....	.....	.....	...	...	...	.....	.....	2	11	0	1.000
1916—Shreveport	Tex.	P	19	29	3	7	3	1	0	.....	.241	2	14	3	.842
1917—Shreveport	Tex.	P-OF	95	208	15	48	9	1	4	.....	.231	51	61	9	.926
1918-19-20-21—							(Played semi-pro ball)								
1922-Toledo	A. A.	1B	88	235	41	79	11	4	14	61	.336	417	54	10	.979
1923-Toledo	A. A.	1B	109	427	73	161	22	11	15	82	.377	957	57	7	.993
1923-New York	Nat.	1B	3	7	1	1	0	0	0	0	.143	22	1	0	1.000
1924-New York	Nat.	1B	77	163	26	39	7	2	5	24	.239	325	14	4	.988
1925-New York	Nat.	1B	133	489	75	156	31	6	11	70	.319	1270	77	14	.990
1926-New York	Nat.	1B-OF	98	225	26	65	12	5	5	43	.289	391	31	9	.979
1927-New York	Nat.	1B	150	580	101	189	32	13	20	121	.326	1621	105	12	.993
1928-New York	Nat.	1B	149	568	100	185	36	11	17	101	.326	1584	78	12	.993
1929-New York	Nat.	1B	150	607	103	226	39	5	14	117	.372	1575	111	11	.994
1930-New York	Nat.	1B	154	633	139	254	39	15	23	129	.401	1538	128	17	.990
1931-New York	Nat.	1B	153	611	121	213	43	20	9	112	.349	1411	105	16	.990
1932-New York	Nat.	1B	154	643	124	225	42	11	28	117	.350	1493	137	14	.991
1933-New York	Nat.	1B	123	475	68	153	20	5	6	58	.322	1246	76	11	.992
1934-New York	Nat.	1B	153	602	109	213	30	6	8	83	.354	1592	105	10	.994
1935-New York	Nat.	1B	145	596	91	203	32	8	6	64	.341	1379	99	6	.996
1936-New York	Nat.	1B	79	229	36	71	10	5	2	39	.310	525	41	2	.996
Major League Totals			1721	6428	1120	2193	373	112	154	1078	.341	15972	1108	138	.992

Jimmie Foxx

Year Club	League	Pos.	G.	AB.	R.	H.	2B.	3B.	HR.	RBI.	B.A.	PO.	A.	E.	F.A.
1924—Easton	East.Sh.	C	76	260	33	77	11	2	10	.....	.296	379	73	16	.966
1925—Philadelphia	Amer.	C	10	9	2	6	1	0	0	0	.667	0	0	0	.000
1925—Providence	Int.	C	41	101	12	33	6	3	1	15	.327	75	9	4	.955
1926—Philadelphia	Amer.	C	26	32	8	10	2	1	0	5	.313	19	5	0	1.000
1927—Philadelphia	Amer.	1B	61	130	23	42	6	5	3	20	.323	263	15	7	.975
1928—Philadelphia	Amer.	1B-3B-C	118	400	85	131	29	10	13	79	.328	416	155	17	.971
1929—Philadelphia	Amer.	1B	149	517	123	183	23	9	33	117	.354	1226	74	6	.995
1930—Philadelphia	Amer.	1B	153	562	127	188	33	13	37	156	.335	1362	79	14	.990
1931—Philadelphia	Amer.	1B-3B	139	515	93	150	32	10	30	120	.291	988	104	15	.986
1932—Philadelphia	Amer.	1B-3B	154	585	151	213	33	9	58	169	.364	1338	97	11	.992
1933—Philadelphia	Amer.	1B	149	573	125	204	37	9	48	163	.356	1402	93	15	.990
1934—Philadelphia	Amer.	1B	150	539	120	180	28	6	44	130	.334	1378	85	10	.993
1935—Philadelphia	Amer.	1B-3B-C	147	535	118	185	33	7	36	115	.346	1226	93	4	.997
1936—Boston	Amer.	1B-OF	155	585	130	198	32	8	41	143	.338	1253	76	13	.990
1937—Boston	Amer.	1B	150	569	111	162	24	6	36	127	.285	1287	106	8	.994
1938—Boston	Amer.	1B	149	565	139	197	33	9	50	175	.349	1282	116	19	.987
1939—Boston	Amer.	1B	124	467	130	168	31	10	35	105	.360	1101	91	10	.992
1940—Boston	Amer.	1B-3B-C	144	515	106	153	30	4	36	119	.297	1023	100	10	.991
1941—Boston	Amer.	1B-3B-C	135	487	87	146	27	8	19	105	.300	1162	118	14	.989
1942—Boston	Amer.	1B	30	100	18	27	4	0	5	14	.270	231	34	1	.996
1942—Chicago	Nat.	1B-C	70	205	25	42	8	0	3	19	.205	491	24	9	.983
1943—Chicago	Nat.							(Did not play)							
1944—Chicago	Nat.	C-3B	15	20	0	1	1	0	0	2	.050	9	6	0	1.000
1944—Portsmouth	Pied.	PH-1B	5	2	0	0	0	0	0	0	.000	0	1	0	1.000
1945—Philadelphia	Nat.	1B-3B	89	224	30	60	11	1	7	38	.268	304	54	8	.978
1946—							(Out of Organized Ball)								
1947—St. Petersburg	Fla.Int.	PH	6	6	0	1	...	...	...	...	.167	.....	...	...	....
American League Totals			2143	7685	1696	2543	438	124	524	1862	.331	16957	1441	173	.991
National League Totals			174	449	55	103	20	1	10	59	.229	804	84	17	.981
Major League Totals			2317	8134	1751	2646	458	125	534	1921	.325	17761	1525	190	.990

Hank Greenberg

Year	Club	League	Pos.	G.	AB.	R.	H.	2B.	3B.	HR.	RBI.	B.A.	PO.	A.	E.	F.A.
1930—Hartford	East.		1B	17	56	10	12	1	2	2	6	.214	157	13	2	.988
1930—Raleigh	Pied.		1B	122	452	88	142	26	14	19	93	.314	1052	78	23	.980
1930—Detroit	Amer.		1B	1	1	0	0	0	0	0	0	.000	0	0	0	.000
1931—Evansville	I.I.I.		1B	126	487	88	155	41	10	15	85	.318	1248	84	25	.982
1931—Beaumont	Texas		PH	3	2	0	0	0	0	0	0	.000	0	0	0	.000
1932—Beaumont	Texas		1B	154	600	123	174	31	11	39	131	.290	1437	103	17	.989
1933—Detroit	Amer.		1B	117	449	59	135	33	3	12	87	.301	1133	63	14	.988
1934—Detroit	Amer.		1B	153	593	118	201	63	7	26	139	.339	1454	84	16	.990
1935—Detroit	Amer.		1B	152	619	121	203	46	16	36	170	.328	1437	99	13	.992
1936—Detroit	Amer.		1B	12	46	10	16	6	2	1	16	.348	119	9	1	.992
1937—Detroit	Amer.		1B	154	594	137	200	49	14	40	183	.337	1477	102	13	.992
1938—Detroit	Amer.		1B	155	556	144	175	23	4	58	146	.315	1484	120	14	.991
1939—Detroit	Amer.		1B	138	500	112	156	42	7	33	112	.312	1205	75	9	.993
1940—Detroit	Amer.		OF	148	573	129	195	50	8	41	150	.340	298	14	15	.954
1941—Detroit	Amer.		OF	19	67	12	18	5	1	2	12	.269	32	0	3	.914
1942-43-44—Detroit	Amer.								(In Military Service)							
1945—Detroit	Amer.		OF	78	270	47	84	20	2	13	60	.311	129	3	0	1.000
1946—Detroit	Amer.		1B	142	523	91	145	29	5	44	127	.277	1272	93	15	.989
1947—Pittsburgh	Nat.		1B	125	402	71	100	13	2	25	74	.249	983	79	9	.992
American League Totals				1269	4791	980	1528	366	69	306	1202	.319	10040	662	113	.990
National League Totals				125	402	71	100	13	2	25	74	.249	983	79	9	.992
Major League Totals				1394	5193	1051	1628	379	71	331	1276	.313	11023	741	122	.990

Johnny Mize

Year	Club	League	Pos.	G.	AB.	R.	H.	2B.	3B.	HR.	RBI.	B.A.	PO.	A.	E.	F.A.
1930—Greensboro	Pied.		OF	12	31	5	6	3	0	0	2	.194	10	0	1	.909
1931—Greensboro	Pied.		OF	94	341	69	115	27	1	9	64	.337	130	17	9	.942
1932—Elmira	NYP		OF-1B	106	405	60	132	20	11	8	78	.326	402	20	6	.986
1933—Greensboro	Pied.		1B	98	378	108	136	29	10	22	104	.360	860	51	25	.973
1933—Rochester	Int.		1B	42	159	27	56	11	3	8	32	.352	355	33	5	.987
1934—Rochester	Int.		1B	90	313	49	106	16	1	17	66	.339	694	72	9	.988
1935—Rochester	Int.		1B	65	252	37	80	11	1	12	44	.317	547	41	8	.987
1936—St. Louis	Nat.		1B-OF	126	414	76	136	30	8	19	93	.329	909	67	6	.994
1937—St. Louis	Nat.		1B	145	560	103	204	40	7	25	113	.364	1308	67	17	.988
1938—St. Louis	Nat.		1B	149	531	85	179	34	16	27	102	.337	1297	93	15	.989
1939—St. Louis	Nat.		1B	153	564	104	197	44	14	28	108	.349	1348	90	19	.987
1940—St. Louis	Nat.		1B	155	579	111	182	31	13	43	137	.314	1376	80	14	.990
1941—St. Louis	Nat.		1B	126	473	67	150	39	8	16	100	.317	1157	82	8	.994
1942—New York	Nat.		1B	142	541	97	165	25	7	26	110	.305	1393	74	8	.995
1943-44-45—New York	Nat.								(In Military Service)							
1946—New York	Nat.		1B	101	377	70	127	18	3	22	70	.337	928	83	11	.989
1947—New York	Nat.		1B	154	586	137	177	26	2	51	138	.302	1381	118	6	.996
1948—New York	Nat.		1B	152	560	110	162	26	4	40	125	.289	1359	111	13	.991
1949—New York	Nat.		1B	106	388	59	102	15	0	18	62	.263	906	65	6	.994
1949—New York	Amer.		1B	13	23	4	6	1	0	1	2	.261	47	3	1	.980
1950—Kansas City	A.A.		1B	26	94	18	28	4	0	5	18	.298	205	17	0	1.000
1950—New York	Amer.		1B	90	274	43	76	12	0	25	72	.277	490	31	2	.996
1951—New York	Amer.		1B	113	332	37	86	14	1	10	49	.259	632	44	4	.994
1952—New York	Amer.		1B	78	137	9	36	9	0	4	29	.263	218	18	3	.987
1953—New York	Amer.		1B	81	104	6	26	3	0	4	27	.250	113	7	0	1.000
American League Totals				375	870	99	230	39	1	44	179	.264	1500	103	10	.994
National League Totals				1509	5573	1019	1781	328	82	315	1158	.320	13362	930	123	.991
Major League Totals				1884	6443	1118	2011	367	83	359	1337	.312	14862	1033	133	.992

Gil Hodges

Year	Club	League	Pos.	G.	AB.	R.	H.	2B.	3B.	HR.	RBI.	B.A.	PO.	A.	E.	F.A.
1943—Brooklyn		Nat.	3B	1	2	0	0	0	0	0	0	.000	1	2	2	.600
1943-44-45—Brooklyn		Nat.						(In Military Service)								
1946—Newport News		Pied.	C	129	406	65	113	27	7	8	64	.278	731	90	14	.983
1947—Brooklyn		Nat.	C	28	77	9	12	3	1	1	7	.156	79	12	4	.958
1948—Brooklyn		Nat.	1B-C	134	481	48	120	18	5	11	70	.249	990	72	17	.984
1949—Brooklyn		Nat.	1B	156	596	94	170	23	4	23	115	.285	1336	80	7	.995
1950—Brooklyn		Nat.	1B	153	561	98	159	26	2	32	113	.283	1273	100	8	.994
1951—Brooklyn		Nat.	1B	158	582	118	156	25	3	40	103	.268	1365	126	12	.992
1952—Brooklyn		Nat.	1B	153	508	87	129	27	1	32	102	.254	1322	116	11	.992
1953—Brooklyn		Nat.	1B-OF	141	520	101	157	22	7	31	122	.302	1062	101	9	.992
1954—Brooklyn		Nat.	1B	154	579	106	176	23	5	42	130	.304	1381	132	7	.995
1955—Brooklyn		Nat.	1B-OF	150	546	75	158	24	5	27	102	.289	1291	106	14	.990
1956—Brooklyn		Nat.	1-O-C	153	550	86	146	29	4	32	87	.265	1234	103	12	.991
1957—Brooklyn		Nat.	1-3-2B	150	579	94	173	28	7	27	98	.299	1319	117	14	.990
1958—Los Angeles		Nat.	1-3-O-C	141	475	68	123	15	1	22	64	.259	932	103	9	.991
1959—Los Angeles		Nat.	1B-3B	124	413	57	114	19	2	25	80	.276	896	74	8	.992
1960—Los Angeles		Nat.	1B-3B	101	197	22	39	8	1	8	30	.198	411	44	5	.989
1961—Los Angeles		Nat.	1B	109	215	25	52	4	0	8	31	.242	454	37	1	.998
1962—New York		Nat.	1B	54	127	15	32	1	0	9	17	.252	315	32	5	.986
1963—New York		Nat.	1B	11	22	2	5	0	0	0	3	.227	61	8	0	1.000
Major League Totals				2071	7030	1105	1921	295	48	370	1274	.273	15722	1365	145	.992

Ted Kluszewski

Year	Club	League	Pos.	G.	AB.	R.	H.	2B.	3B.	HR.	RBI.	B.A.	PO.	A.	E.	F.A.
1946—Columbia		Sally	1B-OF	90	335	59	118	24	5	11	87	.352	525	20	15	.973
1947—Cincinnati		Nat.	1B	9	10	1	1	0	0	0	2	.100	10	0	0	1.000
1947—Memphis		South.	1B	115	427	80	161	32	9	7	68	.377	931	60	19	.981
1948—Cincinnati		Nat.	1B	113	379	49	104	23	4	12	57	.274	833	65	9	.990
1949—Cincinnati		Nat.	1B	136	531	63	164	26	2	8	68	.309	1140	65	14	.989
1950—Cincinnati		Nat.	1B	134	538	76	165	37	0	25	111	.307	1123	61	15	.987
1951—Cincinnati		Nat.	1B	154	607	74	157	35	2	13	77	.259	1381	88	5	.997
1952—Cincinnati		Nat.	1B	135	497	62	159	24	11	16	86	.320	1121	66	8	.993
1953—Cincinnati		Nat.	1B	149	570	97	180	25	0	40	108	.316	1285	58	7	.995
1954—Cincinnati		Nat.	1B	149	573	104	187	28	3	49	141	.326	1237	101	5	.996
1955—Cincinnati		Nat.	1B	153	612	116	192	25	0	47	113	.314	1388	86	8	.995
1956—Cincinnati		Nat.	1B	138	517	91	156	14	1	35	102	.302	1166	89	13	.990
1957—Cincinnati		Nat.	1B	69	127	12	34	7	0	6	21	.268	161	15	2	.989
1958—Pittsburgh		Nat.	1B	100	301	29	88	13	4	4	37	.292	591	36	4	.994
1959—Pittsburgh		Nat.	1B	60	122	11	32	10	1	2	17	.262	151	12	0	1.000
1959—Chicago		Amer.	1B	31	101	11	30	2	1	2	10	.297	220	10	0	1.000
1960—Chicago		Amer.	1B	81	181	20	53	9	0	5	39	.293	325	19	1	.997
1961—Los Angeles		Amer.	1B	107	263	32	64	12	0	15	39	.243	520	28	6	.989
American League Totals				219	545	63	147	23	1	22	88	.270	1065	57	7	.994
National League Totals				1499	5384	785	1619	267	28	257	940	.301	11587	742	90	.993
Major League Totals				1718	5929	848	1766	290	29	279	1028	.298	12652	799	97	.993

Orlando Cepeda

Year	Club	League	Pos.	G.	AB.	R.	H.	2B.	3B.	HR.	RBI.	B.A.	PO.	A.	E.	F.A.
1955—Salem	Appal.	3B	26	93	12	23	6	1	1	16	.247	33	49	16	.837
1955—Kokomo	M.-O.V.	3B	92	374	83	147	23	2	21	91	.393	93	158	27	.903
1956—St. Cloud	North.	1B-3B	125	499	100	177	33	9	26	112	.355	.958	106	26	.976
1957—Minneapolis	A.A.	1B-3B-OF	151	563	91	174	31	3	25	108	.309	1162	103	18	.986
1958—San Francisco	Nat.	1B	148	603	88	188	38	4	25	96	.312	1322	97	16	.989
1959—San Francisco	Nat.	1B-OF-3B	151	605	92	192	35	4	27	105	.317	995	74	22	.980
1960—San Francisco	Nat.	OF-1B	151	569	81	169	36	3	24	96	.297	681	37	13	.982
1961—San Francisco	Nat.	1B-OF	152	585	105	182	28	4	46	142	.311	774	51	5	.994
1962—San Francisco	Nat.	1B-OF	162	625	105	191	26	1	35	114	.306	1356	88	14	.990
1963—San Francisco	Nat.	1B-OF	156	579	100	183	33	4	34	97	.316	1262	83	21	.985
1964—San Francisco	Nat.	1B-OF	142	529	75	161	27	2	31	97	.304	1211	80	18	.986
1965—San Francisco	Nat.	1B-OF	33	34	1	6	1	0	1	5	.176	28	2	0	1.000
1966—S.F.-St. Louis	Nat.	1B-OF	142	501	70	151	26	0	20	73	.301	1171	63	15	.988
1967—St. Louis	Nat.	1B	151	563	91	183	37	0	25	111	.325	1304	90	10	.993
1968—St. Louis	Nat.	1B	157	600	71	149	26	2	16	73	.248	1362	90	17	.988
1969—Atlanta	Nat.	1B	154	573	74	147	28	2	22	88	.257	1318	101	9	.994
1970—Atlanta	Nat.	1B	148	567	87	173	33	0	34	111	.305	1288	112	12	.992
1971—Atlanta	Nat.	1B	71	250	31	69	10	1	14	44	.276	586	49	5	.992
1972—Atlanta	Nat.	1B	28	84	6	25	3	0	4	9	.298	171	13	0	1.000
1972—Oakland	Amer.	PH	3	3	0	0	0	0	0	0	.000	0	0	0	.000
1973—Boston	Amer.	DH	142	550	51	159	25	0	20	86	.289	0	0	0	.000
1974—Yucatan	Mex.	1B	28	80	7	17	1	0	4	17	.213	19	1	0	1.000
1974—Kansas City	Amer.	DH	33	107	3	23	5	0	1	18	.215	0	0	0	.000
National League Totals			1946	7267	1077	2169	387	27	358	1261	.298	14829	1030	177	.989
American League Totals			178	660	54	182	30	0	21	104	.276	0	0	0	.000
Major League Totals			2124	7927	1131	2351	417	27	379	1365	.297	14829	1030	177	.989

Willie McCovey

Year	Club	League	Pos.	G.	AB.	R.	H.	2B.	3B.	HR.	RBI.	B.A.	PO.	A.	E.	F.A.
1955—Sandersville	Ga. St.	1B	107	410	82	125	24	1	19	113	.305	897	51	23	.976
1956—Danville	Carol.	1B	152	519	119	161	38	8	29	89	.310	1273	87	34	.976
1957—Dallas	Tex.	1B	115	395	63	111	21	9	11	65	.281	960	80	10	.990
1958—Phoenix	P.C.	1B	146	527	91	168	37	10	14	89	.319	1171	69	18	.986
1959—Phoenix	P.C.	1B	95	349	84	130	26	11	29	92	.372	896	43	16	.983
1959—San Francisco	Nat.	1B	52	192	32	68	9	5	13	38	.354	424	29	5	.989
1960—San Francisco	Nat.	1B	101	260	37	62	15	3	13	51	.238	557	39	9	.985
1960—Tacoma	P.C.	1B	17	63	14	18	1	2	3	16	.286	149	4	3	.980
1961—San Francisco	Nat.	1B	106	328	59	89	12	3	18	50	.271	669	55	11	.985
1962—San Francisco	Nat.	OF-1B	91	229	41	67	6	1	20	54	.293	186	9	3	.985
1963—San Francisco	Nat.	OF-1B	152	564	103	158	19	5	44	102	.280	363	21	15	.962
1964—San Francisco	Nat.	OF-1B	130	364	55	80	14	1	18	54	.220	273	19	14	.954
1965—San Francisco	Nat.	1B	160	540	93	149	17	4	39	92	.276	1310	87	13	.991
1966—San Francisco	Nat.	1B	150	502	85	148	26	6	36	96	.295	1287	81	22	.984
1967—San Francisco	Nat.	1B	135	456	73	126	17	4	31	91	.276	1221	81	15	.989
1968—San Francisco	Nat.	1B	148	523	81	153	16	4	36	105	.293	1305	103	21	.985
1969—San Francisco	Nat.	1B	149	491	101	157	26	2	45	126	.320	1392	79	12	.992
1970—San Francisco	Nat.	1B	152	495	98	143	39	2	39	126	.289	1217	134	15	.989
1971—San Francisco	Nat.	1B	105	329	45	91	13	0	18	70	.277	828	63	15	.983
1972—San Francisco	Nat.	1B	81	263	30	56	8	0	14	35	.213	617	32	9	.986
1973—San Francisco	Nat.	1B	130	383	52	102	14	3	29	75	.266	930	76	12	.988
1974—San Diego	Nat.	1B	128	344	53	87	19	1	22	63	.253	815	47	11	.987
1975—San Diego	Nat.	1B	122	413	43	104	17	0	23	68	.252	979	73	15	.986
1976—San Diego	Nat.	1B	71	202	20	41	9	0	7	36	.203	420	44	4	.991
1976—Oakland	Amer.	DH	11	24	0	5	0	0	0	0	.208	0	0	0	.000
1977—San Francisco	Nat.	1B	141	478	54	134	21	0	28	86	.280	1072	60	13	.989
1978—San Francisco	Nat.	1B	108	351	32	80	19	2	12	64	.228	721	44	10	.987
1979—San Francisco	Nat.	1B	117	353	34	88	9	0	15	57	.249	740	48	10	.987
1980—San Francisco	Nat.	1B-PH	48	113	8	23	8	0	1	16	.204	241	12	2	.992
National League Totals			2577	8173	1229	2206	353	46	521	1555	.270	17567	1236	256	.987
American League Totals			11	24	0	5	0	0	0	0	.208	0	0	0	.000
Major League Totals			2588	8197	1229	2211	353	46	521	1555	.270	17567	1236	256	.987

Steve Garvey

Year Club	League	Pos.	G.	AB.	R.	H.	2B.	3B.	HR.	RBI.	B.A.	PO.	A.	E.	F.A.
1968—Ogden ....Pion.		3B	62	216	49	73	12	3	20	59	.338	51	109	23	.874
1969—Albuquerque ....Texas		3B-1B	83	316	51	118	18	2	14	85	.373	348	86	20	.956
1969—Los Angeles ....Nat.		PH	3	3	0	1	0	0	0	0	.333	0	0	0	.000
1970—Spokane..................P.C.		3B-2B-OF	95	376	71	120	26	5	15	87	.319	103	178	26	.915
1970—Los Angeles ....Nat.		3B-2B	34	93	8	25	5	0	1	6	.269	23	59	5	.943
1971—Los Angeles ....Nat.		3B	81	225	27	51	12	1	7	26	.227	53	161	14	.939
1972—Los Angeles ....Nat.		3B-1B	96	294	36	79	14	2	9	30	.269	104	189	28	.913
1973—Los Angeles ....Nat.		1B-OF	114	349	37	106	17	3	8	50	.304	731	27	7	.991
1974—Los Angeles ....Nat.		1B	156	642	95	200	32	3	21	111	.312	1536	62	8	.995
1975—Los Angeles ....Nat.		1B	160	659	85	210	38	6	18	95	.319	1500	77	8	.995
1976—Los Angeles ....Nat.		1B	162	631	85	200	37	4	13	80	.317	1583	67	3	.998
1977—Los Angeles ....Nat.		1B	162	646	91	192	25	3	33	115	.297	1606	55	8	.995
1978—Los Angeles ....Nat.		1B	162	639	89	202	36	9	21	113	.316	1546	74	9	.994
1979—Los Angeles ....Nat.		1B	162	648	92	204	32	1	28	110	.315	1402	93	7	.995
1980—Los Angeles ....Nat.		1B	163	658	78	200	27	1	26	106	.304	1502	112	6	.996
1981—Los Angeles ....Nat.		1B	110	431	63	122	23	1	10	64	.283	1019	55	1	.999
1982—Los Angeles ....Nat.		1B	162	625	66	176	35	1	16	86	.282	1539	111	8	.995
1983—San Diego.................Nat.		1B	100	388	76	114	22	0	14	59	.294	888	49	6	.994
1984—San Diego.................Nat.		1B	161	617	72	175	27	2	8	86	.284	1232	87	0	1.000
1985—San Diego.................Nat.		1B	162	654	80	184	34	6	17	81	.281	1442	92	5	.997
1986—San Diego.................Nat.		1B	155	557	58	142	22	0	21	81	.255	1160	53	7	.994
Major League Totals—18 Years			2305	8759	1138	2583	438	43	271	1299	.295	18866	1423	130	.994

Cecil Cooper

Year Club	League	Pos.	G.	AB.	R.	H.	2B.	3B.	HR.	RBI.	B.A.	PO.	A.	E.	F.A.
1968—Jamestown ....NYP		1B	26	84	16	38	6	0	0	6	.452	130	0	1	.992
1969—Greenville................W. Car.		1B-OF	62	212	27	63	12	2	1	18	.297	434	32	8	.983
1970—Danville...................Midw.		1B-OF	114	420	86	141	16	8	3	39	.336	535	33	12	.979
1971—Winston-Salem ....Carol.		1B	42	153	31	58	6	3	6	26	.379	359	21	5	.987
1971—Pawtucket ....East.		1B-OF	98	367	55	126	21	2	10	60	.343	740	35	12	.985
1971—Boston......................Amer.		1B	14	42	9	13	4	1	0	3	.310	82	3	1	.988
1972—Louisville ....Int.		1B	134	515	86	162	31	9	10	78	.315	1102	78	17	.986
1972—Boston......................Amer.		1B	12	17	0	4	1	0	0	2	.235	19	0	0	1.000
1973—Pawtucket ....Int.		1B	128	450	68	132	27	1	15	77	.293	1082	84	12	.990
1973—Boston......................Amer.		1B	30	101	12	24	2	0	3	11	.238	227	17	4	.984
1974—Boston......................Amer.		1B	121	414	55	114	24	1	8	43	.275	637	40	12	.983
1975—Boston......................Amer.		1B	106	305	49	95	17	6	14	44	.311	197	20	1	.995
1976—Boston......................Amer.		1B	123	451	66	127	22	6	15	78	.282	600	42	4	.994
1977—Milwaukee ....Amer.		1B	160	643	86	193	31	7	20	78	.300	1386	118	12	.992
1978—Milwaukee ....Amer.		1B	107	407	60	127	23	2	13	54	.312	842	66	11	.988
1979—Milwaukee ....Amer.		1B	150	590	83	182	44	1	24	106	.308	1323	78	10	.993
1980—Milwaukee ....Amer.		1B	153	622	96	219	33	4	25	122	.352	1336	106	5	.997
1981—Milwaukee ....Amer.		1B	106	416	70	133	35	1	12	60	.320	987	72	9	.992
1982—Milwaukee ....Amer.		1B	155	654	104	205	38	3	32	121	.313	1428	98	5	.997
1983—Milwaukee ....Amer.		1B	160	661	106	203	37	3	30	126	.307	1452	87	11	.993
1984—Milwaukee ....Amer.		1B	148	603	63	166	28	3	11	67	.275	1061	98	10	.991
1985—Milwaukee ....Amer.		1B	154	631	82	185	39	8	16	99	.293	1087	94	17	.986
1986—Milwaukee ....Amer.		1B	134	542	46	140	24	1	12	75	.258	697	61	9	.988
Major League Totals—16 Years			1833	7099	987	2130	402	47	235	1089	.300	13361	1000	121	.992

Keith Hernandez

Year Club	League	Pos.	G.	AB.	R.	H.	2B.	3B.	HR.	RBI.	B.A.	PO.	A.	E.	F.A.
1972—St. Petersburg	Fla. St.	1B	84	309	38	79	16	5	5	41	.256	682	52	7	.991
1972—Tulsa	A. A.	1B	11	29	5	7	1	0	0	1	.241	54	2	0	1.000
1973—Arkansas	Texas	1B	105	388	62	101	20	2	3	52	.260	960	61	9	.991
1973—Tulsa	A. A.	1B	31	120	20	40	6	1	5	25	.333	289	15	1	.997
1974—Tulsa	A. A.	1B-OF	102	353	67	124	18	6	14	63	.351	690	50	12	.984
1974—St. Louis	Nat.	1B	14	34	3	10	1	2	0	2	.294	70	1	2	.973
1975—Tulsa	A. A.	1B-OF	85	324	70	107	29	3	10	48	.330	597	53	13	.980
1975—St. Louis	Nat.	1B	64	188	20	47	8	2	3	20	.250	469	36	2	.996
1976—St. Louis	Nat.	1B	129	374	54	108	21	5	7	46	.289	862	107	10	.990
1977—St. Louis	Nat.	1B	161	560	90	163	41	4	15	91	.291	1453	106	12	.992
1978—St. Louis	Nat.	1B	159	542	90	138	32	4	11	64	.255	1436	96	10	.994
1979—St. Louis	Nat.	1B	161	610	116	210	48	11	11	105	.344	1489	146	8	.995
1980—St. Louis	Nat.	1B	159	595	111	191	39	8	16	99	.321	1572	115	9	.995
1981—St. Louis	Nat.	1B-OF	103	376	65	115	27	4	8	48	.306	1056	86	3	.997
1982—St. Louis	Nat.	1B-OF	160	579	79	173	33	6	7	94	.299	1591	135	11	.994
1983—St.L.-N.Y.	Nat.	1B	150	538	77	160	23	7	12	63	.297	1418	147	13	.992
1984—New York	Nat.	1B	154	550	83	171	31	0	15	94	.311	1214	142	8	.994
1985—New York	Nat.	1B	158	593	87	183	34	4	10	91	.309	1310	139	4	.997
1986—New York	Nat.	1B	149	551	94	171	34	1	13	83	.310	1199	149	5	.996
Major League Totals—13 Years			1721	6090	969	1840	372	58	128	900	.302	15139	1405	97	.994

Eddie Murray

Year Club	League	Pos.	G.	AB.	R.	H.	2B.	3B.	HR.	RBI.	B.A.	PO.	A.	E.	F.A.
1973—Bluefield	Appal.	1B	50	188	34	54	6	0	11	32	.287	421	14	13	.971
1974—Miami	Fla. St.	1B	131	460	64	133	29	7	12	63	.289	1114	51	25	.979
1974—Asheville	South.	1B	2	7	1	2	2	0	0	2	.286	17	0	0	1.000
1975—Asheville	South.	1B-3B	124	436	66	115	13	5	17	68	.264	637	58	15	.979
1976—Charlotte	South.	1B	88	299	46	89	15	2	12	46	.298	746	45	9	.989
1976—Rochester	Int.	1B-OF-3B	54	168	35	46	6	2	11	40	.274	291	13	5	.984
1977—Baltimore	Amer.	OF-1B	160	611	81	173	29	2	27	88	.283	482	20	4	.992
1978—Baltimore	Amer.	1B-3B	161	610	85	174	32	3	27	95	.285	1507	112	6	.996
1979—Baltimore	Amer.	1B	159	606	90	179	30	2	25	99	.295	1456	107	10	.994
1980—Baltimore	Amer.	1B	158	621	100	186	36	2	32	116	.300	1369	107	9	.994
1981—Baltimore	Amer.	1B	99	378	57	111	21	2	22	78	.294	899	91	1	.999
1982—Baltimore	Amer.	1B	151	550	87	174	30	1	32	110	.316	1269	97	4	.997
1983—Baltimore	Amer.	1B	156	582	115	178	30	3	33	111	.306	1393	114	10	.993
1984—Baltimore	Amer.	1B	162	588	97	180	26	3	29	110	.306	1538	143	13	.992
1985—Baltimore	Amer.	1B	156	583	111	173	37	1	31	124	.297	1338	152	19	.987
1986—Baltimore	Amer.	1B	137	495	61	151	25	1	17	84	.305	1045	88	13	.989
Major League Totals—10 Years			1499	5624	884	1679	296	20	275	1015	.299	12296	1001	89	.993

Don Mattingly

Year Club	League	Pos.	G.	AB.	R.	H.	2B.	3B.	HR.	RBI.	B.A.	PO.	A.	E.	F.A.
1979—Oneonta	NYP	OF-1B	53	166	20	58	10	2	3	31	.349	29	2	2	.939
1980—Greensboro	S. Atl.	OF-1B	133	494	92	177	32	5	9	105	.358	205	16	8	.976
1981—Nashville	South.	OF-1B	141	547	74	173	35	4	7	98	.316	846	69	12	.987
1982—Columbus	Int.	OF-1B	130	476	67	150	24	2	10	75	.315	271	17	5	.983
1982—New York	Amer.	OF-1B	7	12	0	2	0	0	0	1	.167	15	1	0	1.000
1983—New York	Amer.	OF-1B-2B	91	279	34	79	15	4	4	32	.283	350	15	3	.992
1983—Columbus	Int.	1B-OF	43	159	35	54	11	3	8	37	.340	325	29	1	.997
1984—New York	Amer.	1B-OF	153	603	91	207	44	2	23	110	.343	1143	126	6	.995
1985—New York	Amer.	1B	159	652	107	211	48	3	35	145	.324	1318	87	7	.995
1986—New York	Amer.	1B-3B	162	677	117	238	53	2	31	113	.352	1378	111	7	.995
Major League Totals—5 Years			572	2223	349	737	160	11	93	401	.332	4204	340	23	.995

INDEX

143